beaded jewellery

beaded jewellery

step-by-step techniques
and projects to create your
own style

maya brenner

DK

LONDON, NEW YORK, MELBOURNE,
MUNICH and DELHI

Project Editor **Betsy Hosegood**
Project Art Editor **Miranda Harvey**
Designer **Kathy Gammon**
Senior Editor **Shannon Beatty**
Senior Art Editor **Peggy Sadler**
Managing Editor **Penny Warren**
Managing Art Editor **Marianne Markham**
Publishing Operations Manager **Gillian Roberts**
Creative Publisher **Mary-Clare Jerram**
Art Director **Peter Luff**
Publishing Director **Corinne Roberts**
DTP Designer **Sonia Charbonnier**
Production Controller **Mandy Inness**

First published in Great Britain in
2006 by Dorling Kindersley Limited
80 Strand, London WC2R 0RL
Penguin Group (UK)

A CIP catalogue record for this book is
available from The British Library
ISBN 978-1-4093-8347-5
001-BD295-March/2012
Printed and bound by Hung Hing, China
Colour reproduction by MDP Ltd, UK

Discover more at
www.dk.com

contents

about the author

With thirteen years of experience in the industry, native Californian Maya Brenner brings undeniable talent to her eponymous jewellery collection. Maya Brenner Designs is both simple and classic, bold and modern. The collection is sold online and at stores around the world.

Maya's celebrity clients include Jessica Biel, Penelope Cruz, Rachel Bilson, Cameron Diaz, Reese Witherspoon, Demi Moore, Salma Hayek, Nicole Richie, Rebecca Romijn, Debra Messing, Molly Sims, Lindsay Lohan, Katy Perry, and Teri Hatcher. Her jewellery has been featured on *Friends*, *The Today Show*, *Desperate Housewives*, *American Idol*, *The Bachelor*, and *Sex & The City*.

Maya's coveted jewellery has also been featured in *InStyle*, *Lucky*, *People*, *Cosmopolitan*, *The New York Times* "Style" section, *Glamour*, *Women's Wear Daily*, *Ladies' Home Journal*, *Life & Style*, *Daily Candy*, and *US Weekly*. Articles written about her career have been posted on CNN.com and About.com, and Maya herself has appeared on *Good Day Live*'s "Style File" and the DIY Network.

She also designs for Stella & Dot, a global home party brand that sells the trend setting jewellery that Maya is known for.

In 2002, Maya won Fashion Group International's Rising Star award, joining the ranks of the design industry's most noteworthy talents.

Lately, her main sources of inspiration are her two beautiful children, Jack and Sadie.

for the love of beads

I love beads. A simple bead is the perfect little entity, but when joined together with other beads it can take on a whole new form. It can become muted or bold, colourful or monochromatic. Working with beads provides endless combinations, endless possibilities and endless enjoyment.

Beads are a universal delight. Practically every culture has them, be they made from animal teeth, fish bones, clay or stones, and as the culture develops so too do the beads. There are now such seductive arrays of beads available worldwide that it is only too easy to get totally carried away like a child in a sweet shop.

the right style

Beads are wonderful because they are glamorous, seductive, sparkling, chic, elegant, glorious, fun – whatever you want them to be. It's you who sets the mood through your choice of beads and the way you put them together. Whether you wear jewellery all the time and want something for every occasion or whether you want to make that single perfect item you've always wanted, you can do it with beads – and with pleasure.

the right meaning

Choosing your own beads not only gives you control over styling but also over meaning. What about including a birthstone or sign of the zodiac, for example? Or you could choose stones that are said to have meanings or powers: peridot to attract love and money; coral to protect children and give wisdom; tourmaline for tranquil sleep, and citrine to lift the spirits and soothe the nerves. There are plenty of sites on the Internet where you can find out about these things and plenty of fun to be had making a mystical bracelet. So whatever your interests, whatever your style and whatever your mood, there are beads to fit the bill, and what could be more exciting, inspiring and rewarding than that?

stunning selection
You can buy beads of just about every shape, size and material imaginable. For me, it's impossible to see them and not desire them.

quick fix
You can make a piece in under 30 minutes,
wear it to a party and then dismantle it the next
day and make something entirely different.

why do it yourself?

Making beaded jewellery is a creative, artistic, money-saving, fun hobby with endless possibilities, and if that isn't enough to inspire you then think of all those wonderful presents you can make for family and friends – and even for yourself – and there's no need to look any further.

The number one reason to make jewellery yourself is that it's fun, fun, fun! I always love the instant gratification of sitting down to make a necklace and having something to wear that very night. You can make jewellery to match particular outfits or favourite colour combinations or even to enhance mood and well-being since many semi-precious stones are said to have health-improving qualities.

economy

If you're a jewellery fanatic like I am then you'll find that making your own pieces is a definite money saver once you have got over the initial outlay of buying basic tools and findings. I can't even tally the amount of money I spent on jewellery that I could have made myself for much less. Plus, I could have had it the length and colour that I wanted instead of settling for what was available. What's more, once you learn the techniques you can easily dismantle pieces that you've made and no longer like and turn them into something more fashionable (see pages 212–213), ensuring endless creativity and fun.

Chinese dream
Making your own jewellery enables you to create a piece that's individual to you or tailor-made for a friend.

pastel variation
Although made using the same knotting technique as the piece on the left, this necklace has a whole new look.

where to start

You've already taken the first steps toward making your own beaded jewellery by opening this book and reading it. Now you need to start with something simple and go on from there. The easy projects in this book will teach you the basic skills. After that, the possibilities are endless.

Your starting point for any project is to think about what type of jewellery you'd enjoy and feel comfortable wearing and go from there. Get inspiration from books like this, magazines, jewellery stores, online sites or anywhere that you can view jewellery comfortably.

developing skills

Besides reading this book, another option is to take a class at a local bead store or college. Many schools offer courses in jewellery making and sometimes these are run in the evenings. One of the first classes I took was at the YMCA. I also asked people who worked at bead stores that I frequented to teach me a few skills – I first learned to wire wrap at the counter of a bead store.

getting supplied

Bead stores are popping up across the planet. If there's not one near you, you can order beading supplies online, but I would always recommend buying in person if at all possible so that you can touch and feel the

beads. Also, until you get familiar with sizes and shapes, all the choices can be confusing unless you can actually see them together.

overcoming beader's block

The best way to start is just that – start. Don't worry if your pieces aren't perfect at first. Practise, practise and more practise makes good enough. Believe it or not, some of the most complicated designs are actually quite simple. So good luck and happy beading!

ease of construction

To help you sort out what's really easy and what's not, all the projects in the designer section on pages 84–153 have been graded as follows:

●○○ easy   ●●○ intermediate   ●●● harder

simple
There are plenty of projects for beginners, such as these lovely drop earrings (see page 90).

trickier
Some projects take a little more time and experience, like this bracelet (page 106).

advanced
This stunning necklace, featured on pages 146–149, is an advanced project but the step-by-step instructions break it down into easy sections, so once you have made a few items successfully you'll be ready to try this one.

choosing the right beads

With so many desirable beads out there how can you possibly make a selection? The choice is certainly astounding and it's easy to get confused, so the best plan is to have a distinct idea of what you want to make before you shop so you can limit what you look at. Here are some more tips to help you through.

Budget is always at the heart of any buying experience. Sure, we'd all like to work with rubies, emeralds and diamonds but we've got to be realistic here. If money's really tight don't even glance at the semi-precious section. See what's available in resin, plastic, wood and glass, and consider designs that mix a few really gorgeous focus beads with seed beads or any of the other inexpensive types.

Size & shape relate to the overall design. With every project in this book you'll find a list of the beads I used. You don't have to copy me exactly, but the list will give you an idea of the sizes and shapes that are suitable.

Style is completely a matter of personal preference, so I can't help you here – you already know what you like.

Material affects looks and practicality. Many semi-precious stones can be scratched or broken, so don't choose them for casual items, even if you have the budget. On the other hand they look wonderful and may be the ideal choice for evening wear.

Weight is important too, which is one of the reasons why it is always better to see the beads and to hold them in your hand before you buy. Heavy beads can be uncomfortable to wear, not just in earrings but in necklaces and bracelets too, if you have too many of them.

Colour is the reason why many of us choose the beads we do. A single or two-colour theme nearly always works well, and you can mix beads of all types to suit all budgets. There's nothing wrong with choosing beads this way, though you might want to watch out that you don't make every single piece in the same colour theme!

small & light
Small beads may look insignificant on the counter, but when you put lots together you get something wonderful (see pages 94–95).

large & small
Create variety of scale by combining beads of different sizes (see pages 92–93).

bold & beautiful
These wooden beads are beautiful for their simplicity, and when combined bring out each other's textures and colours. The gold beads add glamour (see pages 130–133).

preparation

about beads

Used by the Ancient Romans and Greeks in their abacuses for counting, as a form of money by traders in the Middle Ages, and by priests and monks to keep track of repeated prayers, beads have held a special place in human lives for many centuries. Today we use them mainly for personal or cultural decoration, and this, too, has been going on since early times as we know from historical finds in Africa and the East. The captivating qualities of beads – their colours, mesmerizing forms and intricacies – continue to enthral and are likely to maintain their place in our hearts for centuries to come.

shape & size

If you haven't been in a bead store yet, you'll be amazed at what's available, not just in terms of colour and type but also at the most basic level – size and shape.

1 Seed beads are most often associated with embroidery but they are great used as spacers between larger beads or in groups (see the projects on pages 112–113 and 150–153).

2 Cones can be used as dangles or strung sideways.

3 Large ornate tubes make wonderful focal beads.

4 The star is a popular bead shape and provides a change of pace.

5 Novelty shapes like these butterflies are great for fun or funky pieces.

6 Drops are ideal for earrings or bracelets (see the Fiesta necklace on pages 134–137). These are made in mirrored crystal.

7 Triangles are unusual without being wacky.

8 The Celtic cross is a popular novelty shape.

9 Some occasions demand something a little out of the ordinary. These starfish would be the perfect accompaniment to a mermaid costume, for example.

10 Small tubes or bugle beads have many uses and fill a string quickly and economically.

11 These square mirrored crystal frames are both unusual and eye-catching.

shape & size

Here are some more different bead shapes to inspire you.

1 Large flat rectangles. These make good focus beads.

2 Small faceted round crystals – some of the most useful beads around.

3 When facets are cut into wood, the change of angle on the grain creates shading, which can look very stylish.

4 Hexagons have a modern look and make a change from traditional round shapes.

5 These flower clusters are unusual. In the right context they could work well.

6 Large flat square beads, like the hexagons and rectangles, offer an elegant alternative to the traditional spherical shape.

7 It's obvious where doughnut beads get their name. These make excellent medallions.

8 This unusual wooden medallion is drilled across one corner so it hangs like a Celtic cross.

9 Looking like wrapped sweets, these puffed squares are made from glass with foil inside. They are drilled on the diagonal for added interest.

10 Both stylish and useful, rice-shaped beads are popular and versatile.

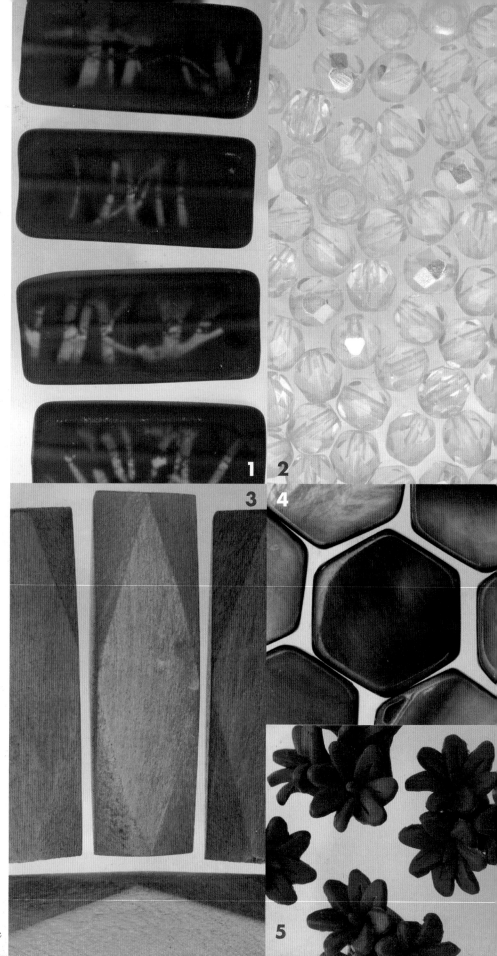

shape & size

Here are a few more beads typical of those available. There are thousands more shapes to choose from but these pages should give you some idea of what's out there.

1 Tube shapes are easy to produce and you'll find lots of beads like this, especially at the cheaper end of the scale.

2 If you want to include semi-precious stones in your jewellery but want to keep the cost down then tumbled chips like these are for you. They have a pleasant natural shaping, as shown.

3 Rondells are like small doughnut shapes and highly useful and versatile.

4 These unusual beads look like black ladybugs and are great fun.

5 Flat ovals are very elegant when made out of a quality material like this mother-of-pearl. They are excellent for classic styling.

6 Medallions have a hole at one end for threading. This one is a shell slice.

7 Another medallion, this time a large square, which makes the most of a beautiful shell.

8 Large wooden wheel shapes with a central hole. Use like a bead or medallion.

9 These bone-effect beads are drilled through the narrow end so the feather hangs down. Buy a pair to make an unusual set of earrings or use one at the centre of a necklace as a focus.

7

8 9

glass

These beads come alive when the light catches them, sparkling enticingly and glowing with colour. They are heavier than plastic or resin but lighter than metal.

1 Large blue barrel-shaped beads work well alongside more decorative versions.

2 A frosted look, sometimes created by adding foil within the bead, gives plain glass added elegance but won't necessarily cost the earth.

3 These large frosted beads could be used as focal points on necklaces or bracelets.

4 Flat, heart-shaped beads are ideal for earrings but can also be used in bracelets and necklaces, though if strung they will be sideways.

5 Twisted threads of glass run over the surface of these beads, providing subtle colour and texture.

6 Mirrored glass has fantastic sparkle and makes the most of any available light, but the beads have definite right and wrong sides so you won't always be able to use them.

7 Frosted glass beads work well together and can be happily combined.

8 Chunky glass beads are excellent for an ethnic look.

9 Large glass balls are inexpensive and you only need a few for a bracelet.

10 Glass seed beads are surprisingly versatile – a must for the beader's store box.

11 White and clear beads go with just about everything. Buy them in a range of sizes and you'll be amazed how soon you run out.

6 7 8 9 10 11

crystal & decorated glass

Whether breathtakingly fabulous or fun and funky, decorated glass and crystal beads are bound to find a space in your bead box. The problem is that they could create a similarly large space in your purse.

1 These funky glass beads are not too expensive and children especially will love their bright colours.

2 The gold foil inside these beads gives them a classy look. They'd be great for the vintage-style bracelet on page 112.

3 Look out for coloured glass in shapes like these if you want your jewellery to stand out from the rest.

4 Real crystal beads glow with intense colour. These drops would make any item look fantastic.

5 Mirrored crystal reflects light like nothing else. These golden hearts are definite attention-grabbers.

6 Not sure which colours to use? Choose beads like these and then select the other beads to match.

7 These flat glass squares have a funky look.

8 You'll only need one or two of these superb focus beads in your piece.

9 Stunning doughnut beads can be used like medallions.

10 These foiled glass cones have a subtle elegance.

11 Small crystal beads can enhance your colour theme. They come in many different colours and sizes.

1 - 2

3   4

5

resin & plastic

These colourful, lightweight beads are the ones many jewellery makers start off with. Often available in economical multi-packs, they are ideal for experimentation and can be combined with similar beads or used to pad out more expensive beads to good effect.

1 These faceted matte yellow beads combine especially well with wood or glass.

2 Bold red acrylic balls will add drama to any piece.

3 Decorative beads like these come in acrylic or glass and add a youthful look.

4 Acrylic can be moulded into many shapes, like these funky flowers.

5 Bright doughnuts can provide a change of pace.

6 These would make wonderful festive jewellery.

7 Some of the fancier bead shapes would be perfect for special occasion pieces, perhaps for a wedding.

8 Bright yellow balls add a little sunshine to a dark day.

9 Mix bright colours together for impact.

10 These unusual flat faceted beads look good enough to eat and are highly versatile.

11 Not all acrylic and plastic beads are bright – this sample shows how useful they are for subtle effects too. Mix these with a few clear crystals for a delicate, shimmering effect, fit for a princess.

metal

Metal beads are some of the most useful around. Use them like spacers to add richness to your work or to highlight special beads or make them the focus of your piece. Be warned, however, some of them are quite heavy, so you don't want to overdo them.

1 Wire beads with hollow centres are lightweight and have a delicate look.

2 These chunky gold-colour beads have an exotic style.

3 Flat gold-colour discs can make unusual focal points.

4 Many metal beads have intricate carvings that add subtle detail.

5 Small faceted metal beads like these have a host of uses. Choose them to match the colour of your clasp.

6 These silver-colour beads have an Indian look. They are available in sterling silver.

7 In complete contrast, these metal beads have an ultra-modern style.

8 Fluted metal beads like these work well in many situations. They are lightweight too, which is a great advantage.

9 You only need a few of these big, chunky hexagons for a bold effect (see the Quick and Easy bracelet shown on page 170).

10 Here's the gold version of No 6. Gold colourings vary, so watch out for this when combining several.

11 Little gold or silver beads like these can be used as spacers on either side of your focal beads.

wood

Wooden beads are available in wonderful muted tones from buff and honey to rich reds browns, greys, and even black. They go well with metals (see page 170) but also combine nicely with semi-precious beads as in the turquoise and coral necklace on pages 146–149.

1 These barrel-like beads will add body to your work.

2 Buff-coloured beads, like these long faceted tubes, go with most styles.

3 Huge wooden doughnuts provide a change of pace.

4 These marquetry beads make excellent focal points.

5 Wooden beads can be stained; do it yourself or buy them ready coloured.

6 Faceted to create a pattern of grey and buff, these are elegant and versatile.

7 Natural wood shades harmonize with just about everything and combine wonderfully with each other (see pages 130–133).

8 These stunning beads make excellent medallions. Try using one as an alternative to the shell in Island Dream (see pages 150–153).

9 Wooden beads work well stained or painted in a bright, hot colour, which enhances the natural warmth of the wood.

5

6 7

8 9

shell

Shell is a wonderfully varied material that can be used to particularly good effect alongside crystal, glass and semi-precious beads. Often available as medallions, they make excellent centrepieces.

1 This shell slice has been drilled as a large medallion. Being quite heavy it is most suitable for a necklace.

2 You can see this large round shell medallion on Island Dream, page 150.

3 Although this shell was bought in a bead store you can find similar specimens on beach holidays, which will make your piece even more special.

4 Mother-of-pearl is a relatively inexpensive shell and is often dyed to produce some lovely colours. Here the combination of the elegant square shape and green colouring makes for some subtle but very chic beads.

5 These creamy mother-of-pearl beads have been cut as flat ovals – a very useful shape for all types of jewellery.

6 Shell combines well with beads that pick up its tints of pink, green or blue.

7 Shell that shimmers with creamy tints is ideal for bridal wear or anytime you want a neutral look that will go with almost anything.

8 The tortoiseshell look of these rectangular medallions has great elegance. See one in use on page 153.

9 Abalone is an expensive shell but its remarkable depth, sheen and blue-green-purple colouring are surely worth it.

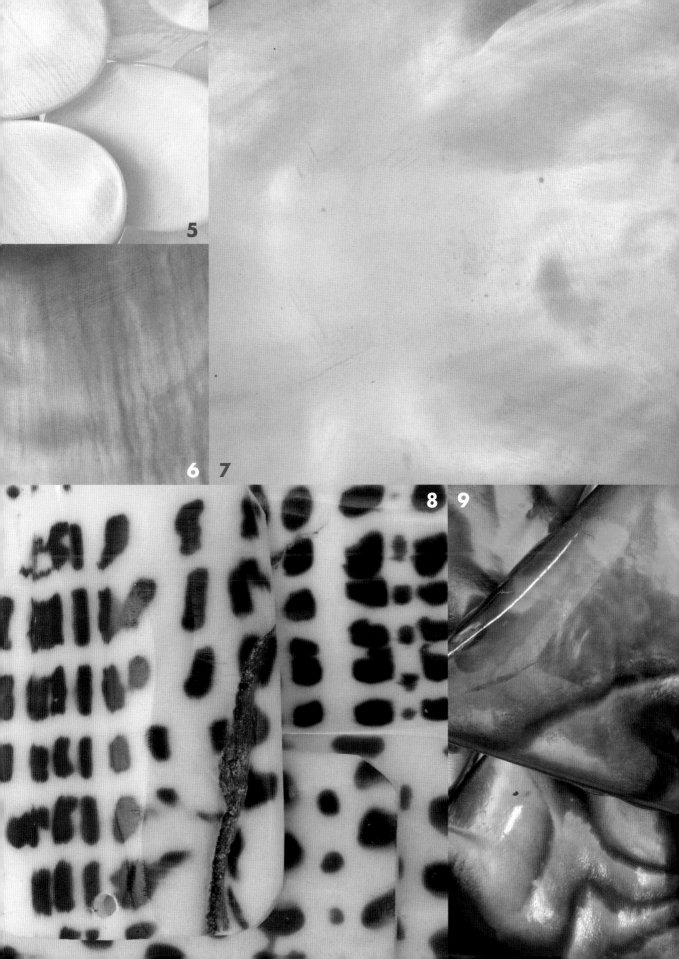

5

6 7

8 9

pearl

At one time every woman or wealthy young lady had at least one pearl necklace and the earrings to go with it. These days, what with freshwater, cultured and fake pearls you don't have to be rich to have them. Choose traditional cream tones for a cultured look or opt for bold or wacky colours for a contemporary feel.

1 Most fake pearls capture the pearlescent quality of the real thing but the colours are often more vibrant.

2 Metallic pearls suit a vampish mood.

3 These small greyish potato pearls will go with just about anything and everything.

4 Choose fake pearls to match an outfit and remember that you can combine them with other bead types to good effect.

5 This unusual colour makes no pretence at being natural but they are so flattering who really cares?

6 In rich cream, these tiny potato pearls look like the real thing but at only a fraction of the cost.

7 Freshwater pearls come in a range of natural hues and have pleasingly irregular shapes. They add a traditional, expensive look to any item of jewellery.

8 Realistic large potato pearls create a classic look.

9 These pink pearls are sure to warm the soul.

10 Look out for pearls with metallic finishes, which are inexpensive but stylish (see page 141).

bone &
lacquer

This category would once have included items such as ivory but, in the same way as pearl, it is now more likely to encompass a large selection of look-alikes.

1 These large rondell or doughnut shapes look great in chunky pieces.

2 With their African designs these tubes work well in ethnic-style jewellery.

3 Red carved lacquer beads have a Far Eastern feel. They are sure to turn a piece into a talking point.

4 These two-colour beads add pattern to your pieces in a fairly subtle way.

5 Like No 4, these beads have a natural look that suits many different styles.

6 This huge flat round bead makes an excellent medallion for a piece with a distinctly Chinese orientation.

7 These large, flat ovals combine several colours, making them quite versatile.

8 Reminiscent of carved wooden flowers seen in Tudor manors, these flat round beads have a nostalgic feel.

9 These carved tubes look like ivory but aren't. Their creamy colour makes them highly useful.

10 These tubes look as if they could be made of wood but their texture is more like bone. Like all the beads in this category they are versatile and becoming.

ceramic, porcelain & enamel

If you want to make a bold statement with your jewellery consider using beads in china or enamel, which, like bone beads, often have an Eastern look. Sometimes these beads can be quite heavy, so it's a good idea to hold them in your hand before you make a selection.

1 These round beads look like traditional blue and white china. Several designs are available, which can be successfully combined.

2 Blue enamel stars perk up earrings and bracelets.

3 These lovely gilded beads look hand painted.

4 You'll find red and green in many of the blue and white china beads, giving you the opportunity to introduce more colour.

5 A rich mottled colour and unusual cube shape make these beads stand out.

6 Flat round enamel beads in a stunning combination of orange-red and turquoise. These are both lightweight and versatile.

7 These small glazed beads have many uses.

8 Some of the lovely glazing effects possible in large-scale pottery can be achieved on beads. These ones are especially wearable.

9 A flat, rectangular version of No 2.

10 With their simple honeycomb pattern these beads have infinite possibilities.

gems & semi-precious stones

Semi-precious and precious stones are at the top end of the bead market, and once you have had some experience of jewellery making you may feel ready to use them. There's no doubt that they will enable you to create stunning pieces.

1 Stone chips, like these carnelians, can be surprisingly economical but they will add that designer look to your work.

2 Aquamarine is said to enhance mind, body and spirit. It's also very pretty.

3 The lovely mottled green of malachite works well with many other gems. It is similar to green jasper and jade.

4 Garnets are often used by professional jewellers in place of more expensive rubies.

5 Turquoise comes in many variations from green to blue. These blue chips are at the paler end of the scale.

6 More turquoise, this time in a mid-range colour that is most closely associated with this stone. These beads have probably been dyed, a common process that stabilizes the stone.

7 Coral comes from the calcified bodies of tiny sea creatures. The amazing range of pinks, peaches and deep reds make this a highly desirable (though endangered) item.

findings & stringings

Findings, such as clasps, pins, rings and ear wires, are all the components used in the construction of jewellery apart from the beads. Also known as fastenings, components and connectors, these little pieces can be as important as the beads in any design. It's easy to think you can skimp on these elements but cheap findings can devalue a piece while the best of them can raise it to exceptional levels. They can change the overall look of a piece too – a clasp can make an item look ornate or plain, vintage or new.

pins, rings & spacers

1 Spacers are small beads used as accents in a design and also to separate larger beads. They are often seed beads or metal, like these daisy spacers.

2 Headpins look like long dressmaker's pins and come in various lengths and thicknesses. When you thread on the beads the flattened end stops them falling off. These are used mostly for earrings and pendants.

3 Jumprings are small oval or round wire rings used to link charms or pendants onto a chain. They are not usually soldered shut so they are easy to open but may also open during wear.

4 Eyepins are similar to headpins but with a loop instead of a flat end. These are used for rosary type designs and longer earrings with multiple beads.

5 Crimp beads are used to secure beading wire to the clasp or other item. Choose a size appropriate to the thickness of the wire.

6 Long silver headpins with decorated ends.

7 Shell ends can be used to cover the knot that joins a string to the clasp.

8 Bead ends or caps are metal ornaments, sometimes filigree, that are used at each end of a glass or stone bead to accentuate it. They can also be used to cover any roughness or damage around the drilled hole.

9 Large gold-colour crimp beads.

10 Silver-colour crimp beads.

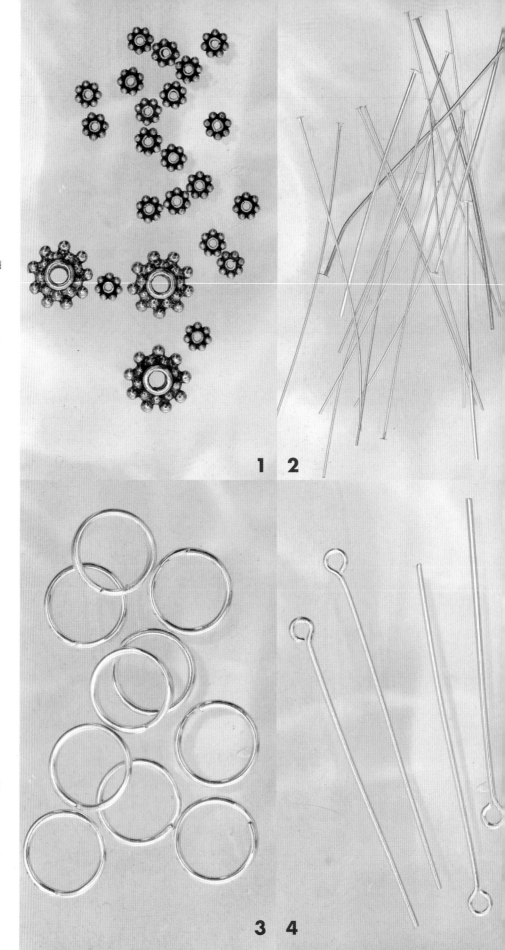

1 **2**

3 **4**

clasps &
ear wires

1 Heart-shaped locks, ideal for charm bracelets.

2 The S-clasp is simple but effective. I like using this clasp when I'm designing with big link chain. You can attach it to any link and it therefore becomes an adjustable-length necklace.

3 A plain silver S-clasp.

4 Lovely silver spring ring clasp with extender chain. Spring ring clasps and lobster clasps can be attached to any link in a chain, making the length easily adjustable.

5 Chunky gold-colour hook and eye clasp.

6 Filigree box clasp popular with classics such as pearls. A small hook, fitted to one end of the strand, slips inside the box and is held in place by tension.

7 Leather ends can be used to finish thongs. Simply press the wrap around the end of the thong and fit the loop to a clasp for a neat finish.

8 Separators secure more than one strand on a multi-strand item. Use them before a clasp or midway through a bracelet or necklace.

9 Large gold-colour barrel clasps. These have two parts that screw together and are unlikely to come undone accidentally.

10 Selection of ear wires.

11 Toggle clasps are perfect for bracelets because you can attach them with one hand — simply pass the bar through the round or oval ring.

12 Large hoops; some are sold complete with ear wire.

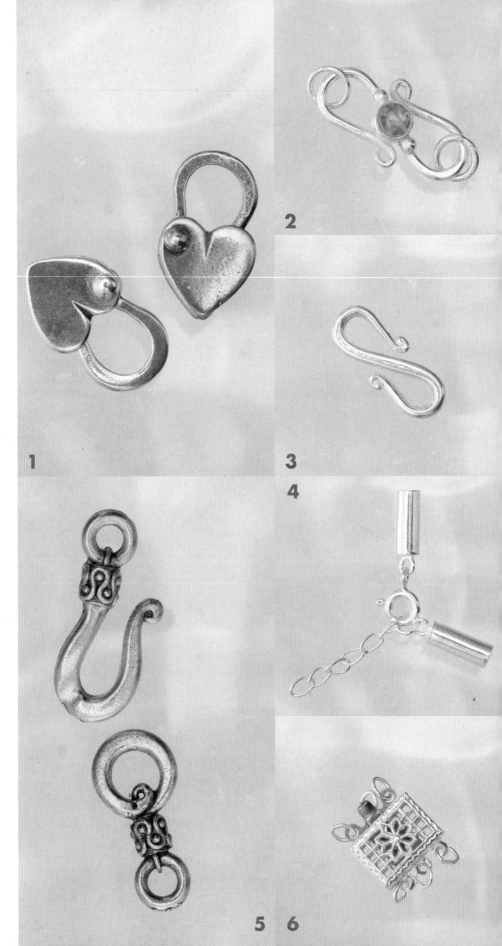

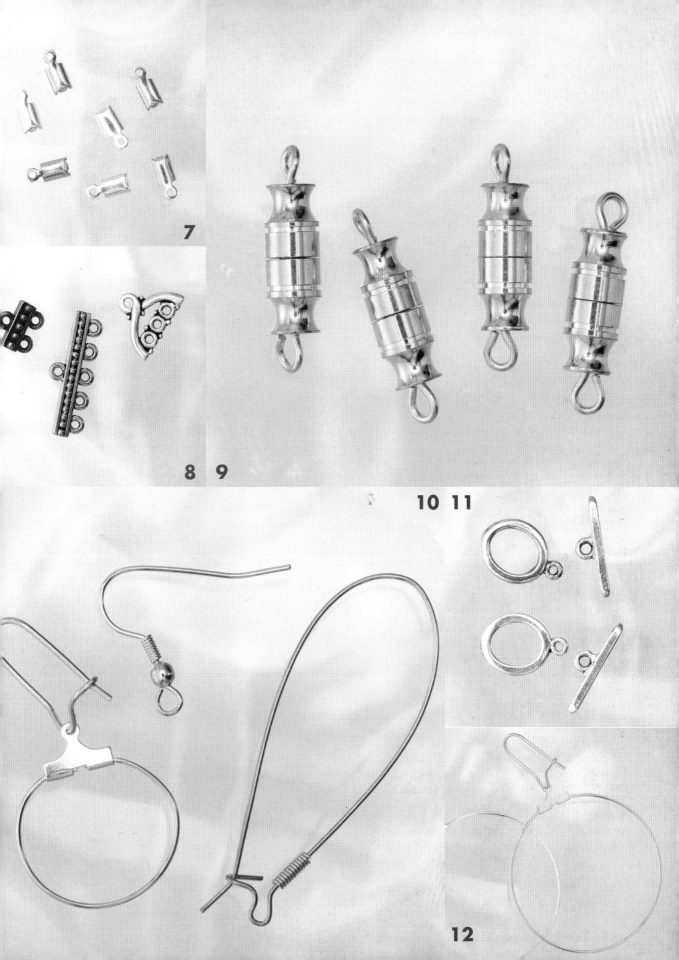

7

8 9

10 11

12

thread & wire

1 "No stretch" thread is a fine, strong stringing thread that comes in about 10 different colours.

2 Thick silk thread is strong and slightly stretchy. It is suitable for medium beads with fairly large holes.

3 Thin silk thread is ideal for pearls and semi-precious beads. Two strands of thread should fit comfortably through the bead without being loose.

4 A variation of No 1. This thread is suitable for small beads of all types.

5 Elastic is ideal for quick bracelets or for children and teenagers. There's no need to add a clasp – just thread on the beads, knot the elastic neatly, trim the ends and it's ready to wear.

6 Silver Soft Flex beading wire comes in several thicknesses. Choose your crimp beads to match.

7 Gold-colour beading wire is ideal where the wire might show. Make sure you use gold-colour findings to match.

8 Wire is needed for wire wrapping. This version is particularly fine.

9 This silk thread comes on a card with a needle or hardened end for easy threading.

10 French wire comes in gold and silver colours and in several thicknesses. It comprises coiled wire and is very delicate. Pass thread through a short piece of French wire to protect it at the clasp (see pages 70–73).

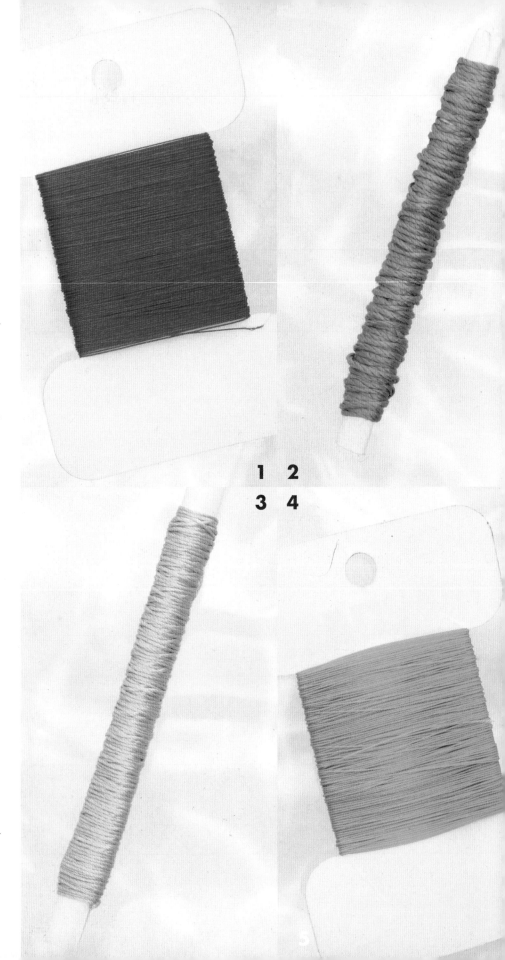

1 2

3 4

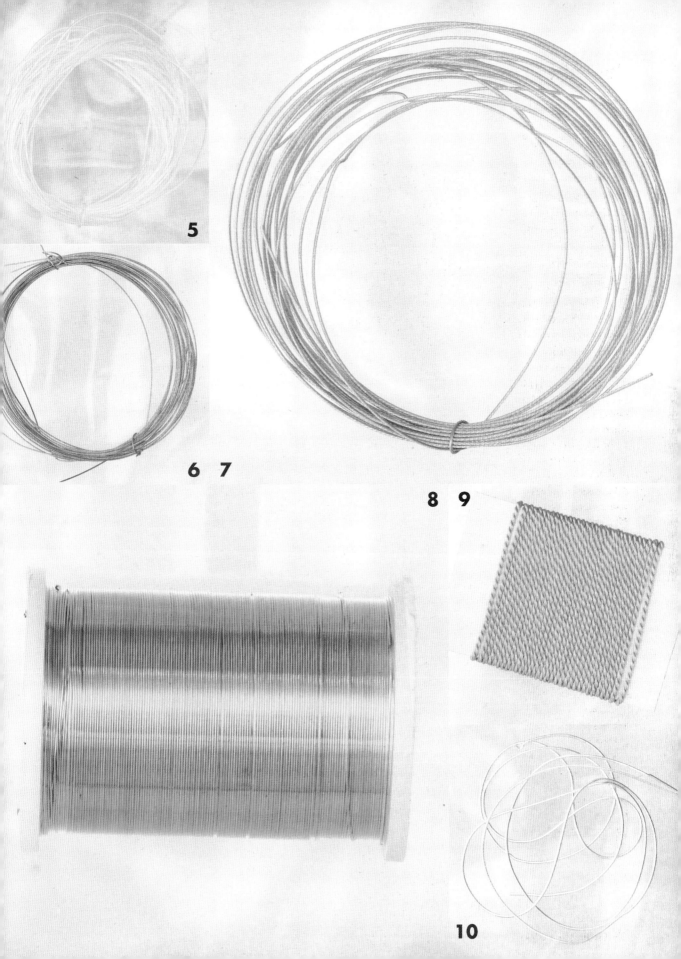

5

6 7

8 9

10

cord &
thongs

Thongs and cords are great
for quick and easy projects
involving large beads.
They have a casual look.

1 Leather thongs come in
several widths and colours
including many natural
shades. They are ideal for
modern pieces where the
thong is a design feature.

2 Softer suede thongs can
be used in the same way as
the leather ones.

3 Fabric cords or rat tails
make a funky alternative to
leather or suede.

4 Wide nylon bands are only
suitable for very chunky
beads or medallions with
large loop fittings or holes.

5 For speed and economy
you can buy thongs with the
clasp already attached. All
you have to do is slip on a
medallion or large bead.

6 Raffia and string can also
be used for beaded jewellery.

7 Metallic thongs are widely
available and ideal for
evening wear.

8 More examples of No 3.
If you can't find the colour
you want, you may be able
to dye a length to match or
complement your beads.

9 Thongs come in many
thicknesses. Make sure your
beads will fit before you buy.

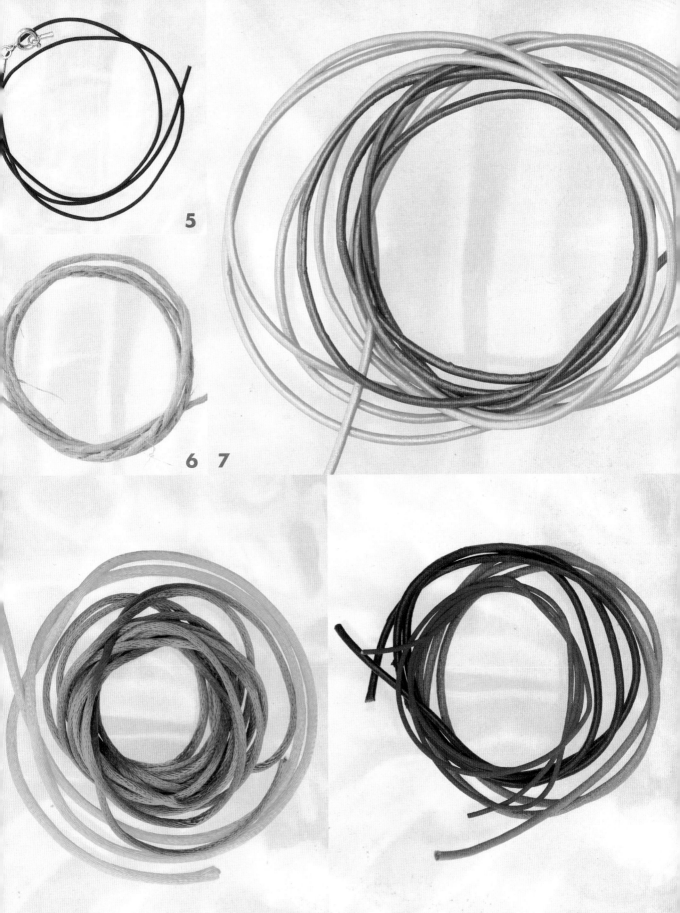

5

6 7

8 9

chain & wire

Chains and chunky or coloured wires are used as features of the design. You'll find a few pieces that use chain in this book.

1 Fine standard gold-colour chain is available in many thicknesses and grades. Make sure your chain is the right weight for your project.

2 Very fine gold chain like this is ideal for dangle or chandelier-style earrings.

3 Oval-link silver chain like this is inexpensive. It could work as a basis for a charm bracelet or necklace.

4 Fine silver chain suitable for earrings and delicate necklaces or bracelets.

5 Silver-colour wire like this is ideal for wire wrapping.

6 Memory wire comes in bracelet and necklace lengths. Simply take the ball off one end and slip on your beads (see pages 166–167).

7 Slinky silver chain with clasp attached. Just add beads or a medallion.

8 Sample packs of funky metal wire are ideal for experimentation and discovery.

9 Some chain is available in colours other than gold or silver, like this black metal.

10 Memory wire for a necklace (see No 6).

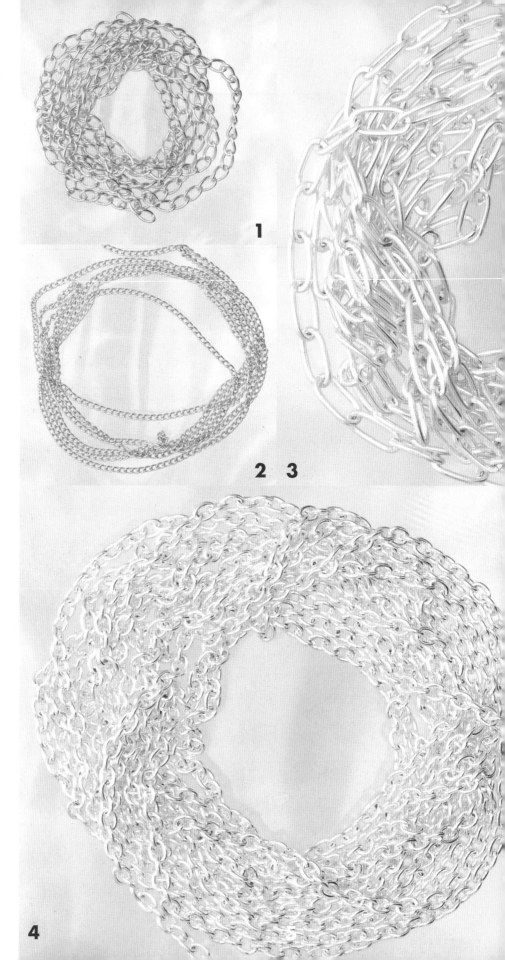

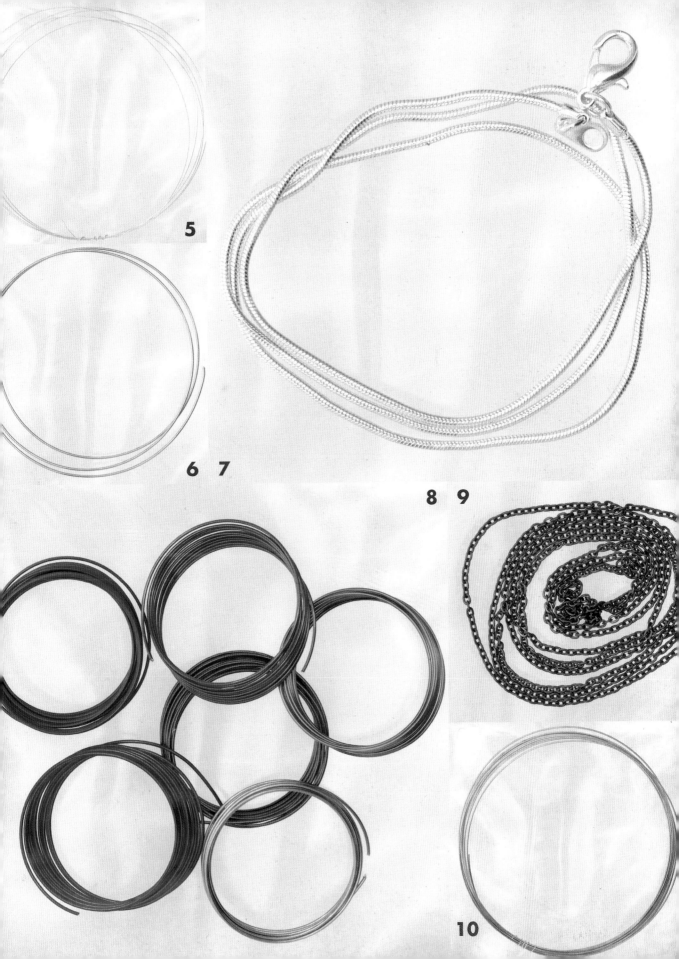

5

6 7

8 9

10

tools

As with all things relating to jewellery making, the tools you use will be a matter of personal preference. The way you were originally taught and by whom may influence which you prefer, and being a leftie or a rightie might determine which tools are most comfortable in your hands. Either way, there's no shortage of tools ranging in price from economy to top quality. Available now are special ergonomic tools designed to avoid some of the carpel tunnel injuries common to repetitive work. On the following pages you'll find some of the most frequently used tools available today.

pliers

Don't think you can get away with using pliers and wire cutters from the shed because you can't. To create neat loops you must have craft pliers, though they needn't cost the earth.

1 Three-step round-nose pliers are designed to help you make the same size of loop again and again, but the flat section can make them awkward to use.

2 Round-nose pliers are necessary for making loops. This is an essential item.

3 Needle-nose pliers have long ends that are flat on the inside and taper to a point. Use them to grasp wire and close crimp beads. If you have a pair of these and a pair of round-nose pliers, you have the basics.

4 Crimping pliers are used specifically for closing crimp beads and do a very nice job. The inner section divides the crimp bead in two to secure the wire firmly on each side.

5 Chain-nose or flat-nose pliers are useful for grasping and pulling wire.

6 Plastic-tipped pliers are gentle on delicate projects but the heads on these are quite thick.

7 Large chain-nose pliers. Choose a size that feels good in your hand and ideally try a few types before you buy.

8 Wire cutters are necessary for cutting the beading wire. Choose a pair with small tips that can reach right up to the crimp beads, like the ones shown here.

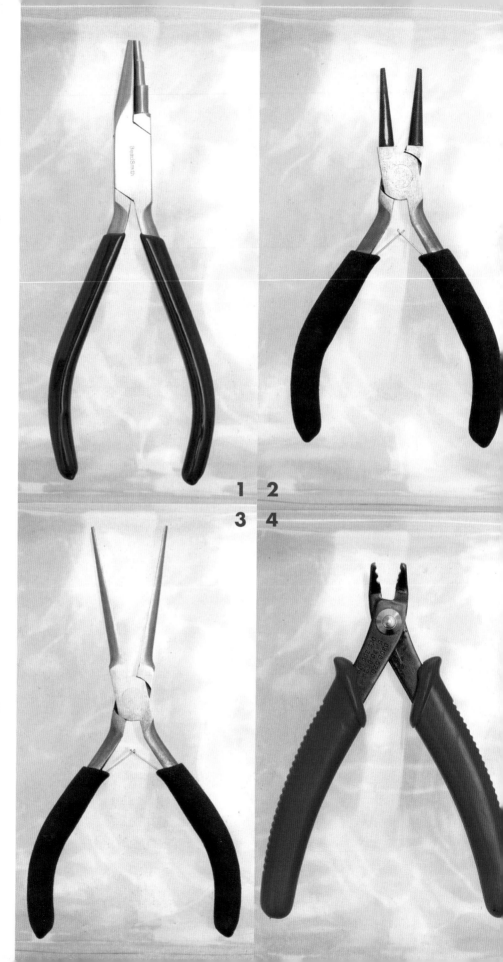

1 2

3 4

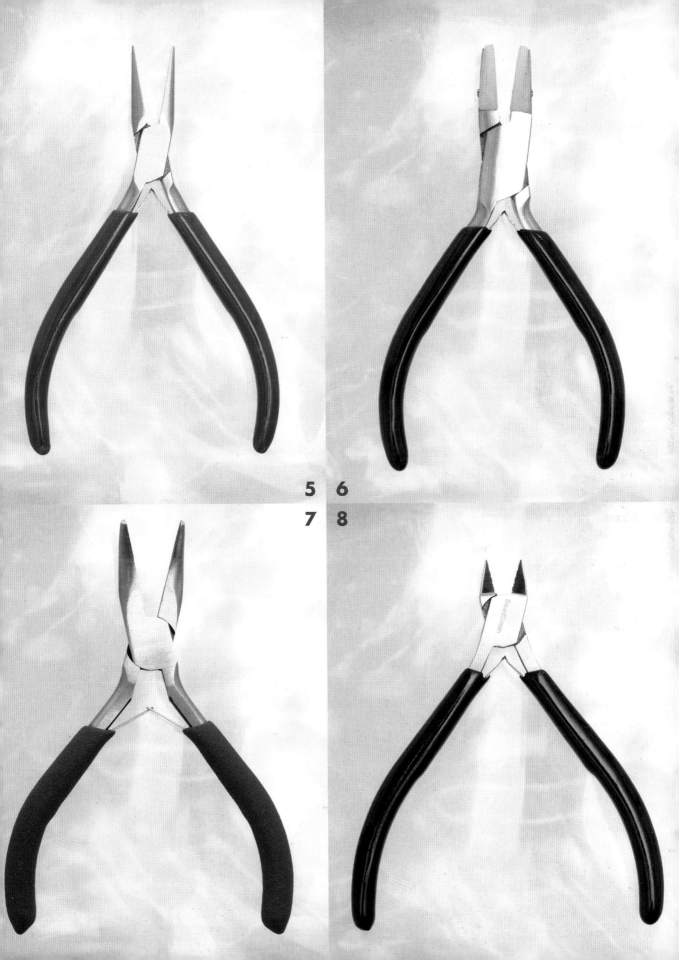

5 6
7 8

other tools

There are a few more items that you may require or want for your jewellery-making projects. You won't need them all at once, and you may never use some of them, so only buy them as you need to.

1 Thread snips are brilliant tools that will cut thread or fine wire close to a knot or crimp bead.

2 Tweezers are needed for knotting (see pages 70–73) and are handy for picking up small beads or securing thread while glue dries.

3 A reamer makes the hole inside a bead a little larger to accommodate your chosen thread or wire.

4 Beading needles are long, narrow and flexible. Choose one with an eye large enough for your thread.

5 This thread cutter can be hung from a cord round your neck so you can always find it when you need to.

6 Beeswax strengthens thread and makes it easier to handle. It's optional.

7 Glues are used to add strength to knots on thread. A long nozzle makes it easier to put it where you want it.

8 A tape measure of some sort is necessary to ensure bracelets and necklaces have the right fit.

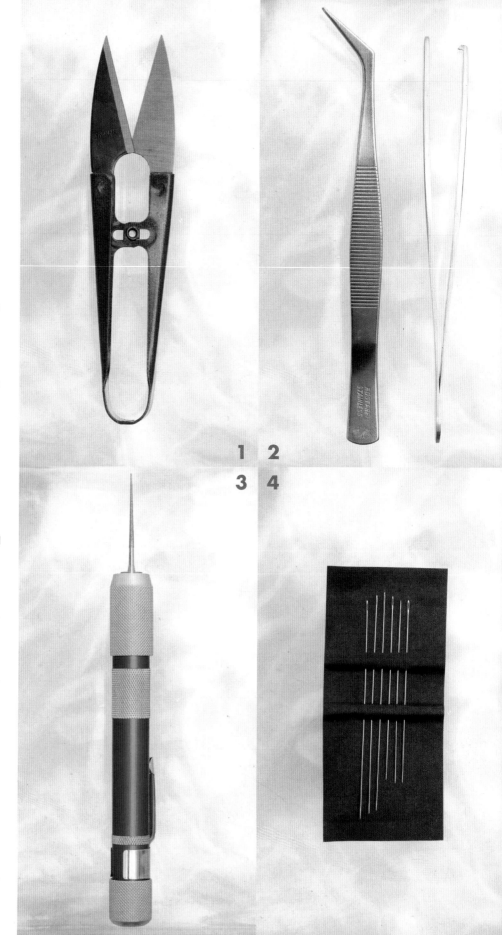

1 2

3 4

5 6
7 8

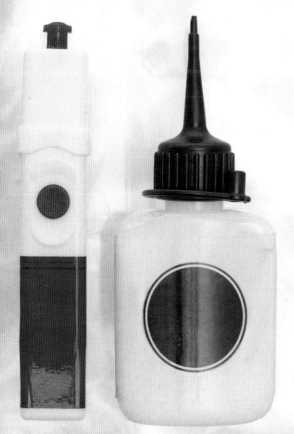

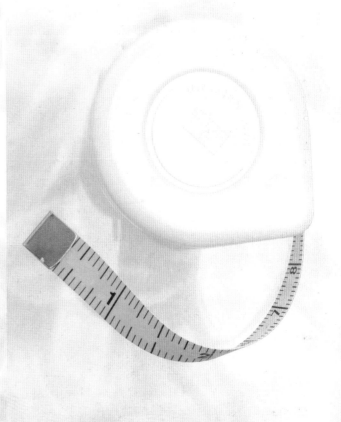

setting up the workplace

Most of us will make our first jewellery at the kitchen table or, if you don't have one of those, you'll do what I did – make it on your bed! However, it makes sense to get yourself set up as well as possible. This will help prevent loss of beads, make working easier and save on some stresses and strains.

Ideally start with a comfortable chair and a flat work surface that will guarantee you're sitting straight. For the surface area, it's best to lay out material on a mat so the beads won't roll around. I sometimes work on dinner plates to keep the beads contained.

Bead boards control the beads while helping with design and stringing. The board's curved groove(s) enable you to arrange beads just as they'll appear around your neck. You can move them around until you are happy with the arrangement. The bead board also has a measuring scale so that you know whether your necklace or bracelet is the right length before you start stringing. Most bead boards also have compartments to hold and sort your beads as you design. There are several different styles of boards available. Inexpensive but functional boards are made from moulded plastic. The best ones have a fuzzy surface applied to the plastic to assist in keeping the beads in place.

Proper lighting is very important for you to be able to see the materials you're working with. If you can, work near a window during the day: natural light is always the best. Or you can use regular overhead lighting. If you find that you're leaning in too much in order to see, try adding a table lamp to your work area.

Bead storage and organization can be made easy with the right bead containers. A good bead storage container is clear to allow viewing without the need to open it. Stacking boxes are great space savers. Small plastic bags have always worked well for me, too, and I usually try to write where I purchased the beads from and how much they cost. This will help later when I price the jewellery or if I need to re-order the beads.

holding areas
Plates and bowls (left) are great for holding your beads while you work because they prevent them rolling away. Long term, store them in sandwich bags or clear plastic containers.

bead board
A bead board (right) stops beads rolling away, enables you to see how a necklace is progressing and even measures it for you as you work.

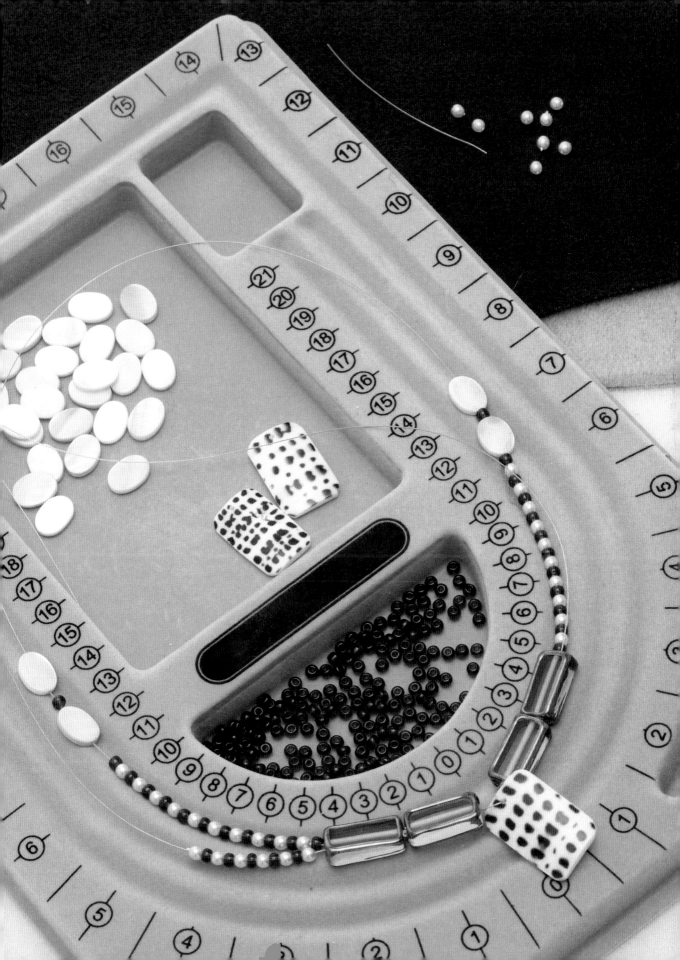

basic techniques

stringing & crimping

Stringing beads and attaching a clasp are essential techniques for nearly all beaded jewellery work. For the crimping you can use special crimping pliers, which are designed specifically for the purpose, or use ordinary needle-nose pliers, which will also do the job effectively.

you will need

tools

Crimping or needle-nose pliers
Wire cutters

materials

Beads for your chosen project

Beading wire such as Soft Flex in a size to fit your beads

Transparent sticky tape

2 crimp beads of a size suitable for your beading wire and in a colour to match the clasp

Clasp of your choice

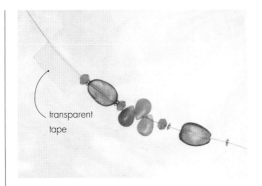

transparent tape

1 Fold a piece of tape over your stringing wire at least 5cm (2in) from the end to prevent the beads falling off. String on your beads. When calculating the desired length, take into account the length of the clasp – you don't want a bracelet slipping off.

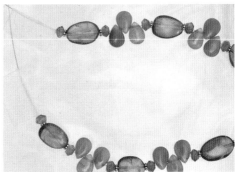

2 When you are happy with the arrangement of beads and the length of the stringing, fold a second piece of tape over the wire, as shown. Never pick up the string unless both ends are taped.

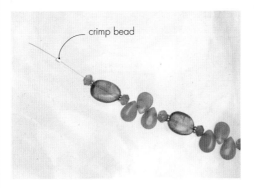

crimp bead

3 Remove the tape from one end of the string and slip on a crimp bead. Slide it down toward the beads.

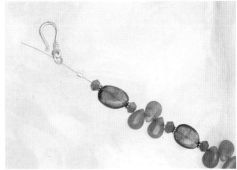

4 Now slide the beading wire through the ring on the clasp. (Your clasp may look quite different from the one shown, but there will be a ring or loop on it somewhere for attaching the beaded string.)

tip

For added security when crimping, pass the wire through the clasp, back through the crimp bead and then on through two or three beads on the string. Crimp as usual and trim the end of the wire. Now slip the end beads back slightly, apply beading glue to the wire and push the beads back up toward the clasp. Now your strand is crimped and glued and definitely won't come apart.

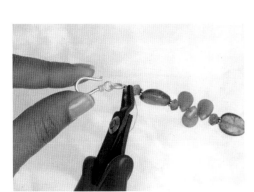

crimp bead

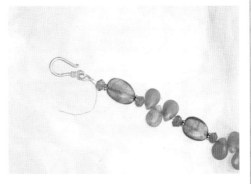

5 Now bend the wire around and pass it back through the crimp bead, as shown. When you start out you may find this process easier if you have extra wire to play with. As you become more experienced you can be more frugal with the wire.

6 Push the crimp bead close to the final bead and pull the end of the wire, drawing the clasp up snugly against the crimp bead. Make sure there are no gaps between the beads at this stage, especially when you come to add the second part of the clasp.

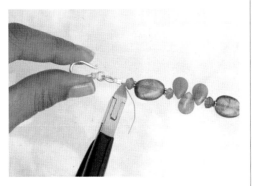

7 Making sure that the clasp and beads are still butted up together, squash the crimp bead firmly using crimping pliers (as shown) or needle-nose pliers. This holds the beading wire in place and secures the clasp.

8 Use wire cutters to cut off the excess beading wire as close as you can to the crimp bead, as shown. Jewellery-making wire cutters have short, shaped blades, which make this process easier. Repeat steps 3–7 to attach the other side of the clasp to the other end of the beaded strand.

knotting a string

A knotted string, in which there is a small knot between each bead or pearl, is not only elegant but practical too. It cushions the beads, preventing them from rubbing and wearing together, which is important when using valuable or soft beads, such as pearls, peridot or aquamarine.

you will need

tools

Stringing needle
Tweezers
Thread snips or scissors
Beading glue

materials

Beads for your chosen project

Silk thread or blended thread to match the predominant bead colour and thin enough for two strands to fit snugly through the beads

French wire large enough to support two thicknesses of the thread in a colour to match your chosen clasp

Clasp

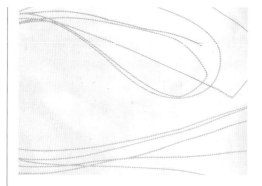

1 Cut your thread so that it is 5–6 times longer than the length of the finished strand. For an 18cm (7in) bracelet you will need 1m (1yd) of silk thread, for example; for a 36cm (14in) choker you will need 2m (2yds).

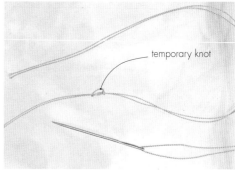

temporary knot

2 Attach your needle and fold the thread in half to create a double strand. Tie the two strands together loosely about 15cm (6in) from the end to prevent the beads slipping off. Alternatively use an alligator clip, which is easy to remove later when you come to add the clasp.

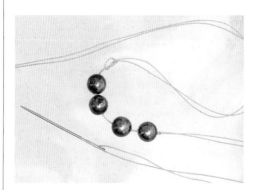

3 Slip on the first four beads without knotting between them. The knots between these beads will be added later, once the clasp has been attached (see steps 11–12).

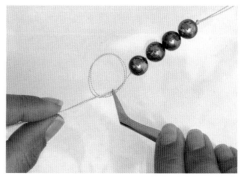

4 Create a loose overhand knot in the thread by making a loop and passing the needle through it. Move the knot along with the tweezers until it is close to the fourth bead, as shown above.

tip

Unfortunately there is no guiding rule to the size of silk thread required for beading because the holes in pearls and semi-precious beads are highly variable. Also the holes are not always consistent and may be wider at the edges than in the centre of the bead. You may need to buy threads in different sizes to find the best fit, and if necessary do some adjustment – if the knots are lost in the holes try using double knots for bulk.

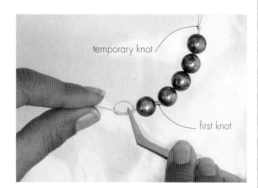

temporary knot

first knot

5 Tighten the knot around the point of your tweezers, pushing the tweezers against the bead. Remove the tweezers. Now use the tweezers to grasp the thread up against the knot and push it gently but firmly toward the bead, as shown, securing it snugly in place.

6 Thread the next bead onto the string and then repeat the knotting process, making sure that the knot is tight up against the bead on each side. This is especially important if you are using silk thread, which stretches.

7 Continue adding beads in the same way, taking your time and making sure all the knots are tight up against the beads. You'll find you get better and quicker with practice. Work until only the last four beads are still to be threaded on the strand.

8 Thread the final four beads onto the strand without knotting between them in the same way as at the beginning. Now you are ready to add the clasp.

tip

French wire is used to prevent the clasp rubbing against the thread and fraying it. It is strong once in place but delicate when handled and if the needle and thread are too large to pass through easily, the French wire can uncoil while you are threading it on. For this reason it is better to buy it too large than too small, so if in doubt buy the largest French wire you can find.

French wire

9 Cut a length of French wire about 12mm (½in) long. This is made from coiled wire and is hollow. Handle it with care to ensure it doesn't uncoil (see the tip, left). Thread it carefully onto your needle and pass it down until it rests against the edge of the final bead.

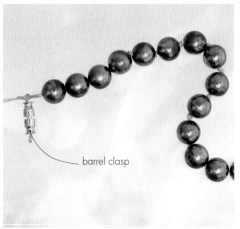

barrel clasp

10 Now slide the clasp onto the French wire, as shown. This clasp is a barrel clasp, but the same technique is used for all sorts of other clasp styles.

French wire

11 Pass the needle back through the last bead on the end of the string. The French wire will fold in half. Pull up the thread so that there is barely enough space to add a knot between each of the four unknotted beads at the end of the strand. Make a knot between the two end beads. This time positioning the knot is easier because there is very little space between the beads.

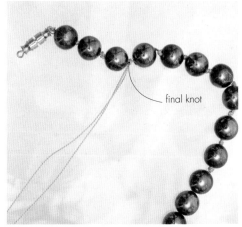

final knot

12 Pass the thread through the second bead from the end and make another knot, then pass it through the third bead and make a final knot on this end of the string.

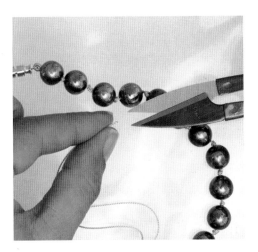

tip

Before cutting off the thread end in step 13 you can pass the thread through the fourth bead from the end and then trim it off. In this way the tiny end of thread is concealed completely inside a bead.

undoing the temporary knot

13 Cut off the thread end close to the beads (see the tip, right). Do this very carefully – you don't want to cut the wrong part! Apply a small drop of glue to each of the knots just made and allow to dry naturally. This provides additional strength.

14 Remove the temporary knot or alligator clip at the other end of the beaded strand so that you can attach the other end of the clasp. You may find it easiest to do this with your tweezers.

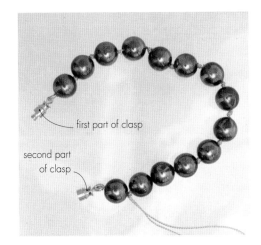

first part of clasp

second part of clasp

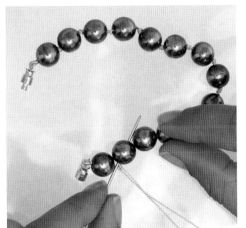

15 Repeat step 9 to add a piece of French wire to the thread. If you are using a barrel clasp, as here, separate the two parts of the clasp and slide the unattached portion onto the French wire. With other clasp styles simply slide on the second part of the clasp. Refer to step 11 to pass the needle back through the first bead and knot between the first and second beads.

16 Repeat steps 12 and 13 on this end of the beaded string to add the remaining knots between the beads. This completes your necklace or bracelet. If you look after it well it will be a lifelong companion. Ideally don't let it get wet, do not store it hanging up and never spray on perfume while wearing it as these can be harmful to the beads and the stringing material.

attaching separators

Separators are used to hold the strands of a multi-strand necklace or bracelet parallel and to add visual impact. These can be placed just before the clasp on each end, as explained here. Other styles of separator can be positioned partway along the beaded strands.

you will need

tools

Wire cutters

Crimping pliers or needle-nose pliers

materials

Soft Flex or equivalent beading wire

Transparent sticky tape

Beads for your chosen project – I used small bugle beads for this demonstration

2 separators to match the clasp suitable for the desired number of strands

2 crimp beads to match the clasp plus 2 more crimp beads for every beaded strand you are using

2 small beads either matching the clasp or the main beads in the piece

Suitable clasp

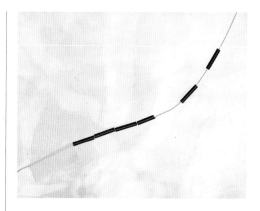

1 Cut the beading wire into the required lengths, allowing an extra 10cm (4in) or more on each one for attaching the clasp using crimp beads. Stick a piece of transparent tape 5cm (2in) from one end of the first piece of wire and begin to string on your beads.

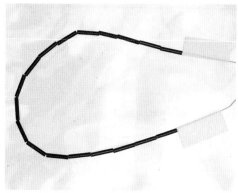

2 Continue to string on the beads until the strand is the required length. (Remember to take into account the length of the clasp and separators when calculating the length of stringing required, see the tip, right.) Add a piece of tape to the other end of the string.

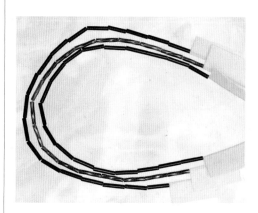

3 Repeat steps 1 and 2 to string up the other strands of beading wire. These strands are the same length for demonstration purposes, but you may wish to make them different lengths.

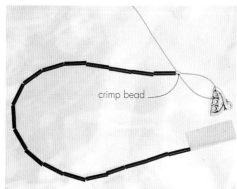

crimp bead

4 Pick up the first/shortest strand and remove the tape from one end. Slip on a crimp bead then pass the wire through the top loop in the separator. Now pass the wire back through the crimp bead, as shown.

tip

Separators are a useful addition to the beader's workbox. Use them wherever you want the strands of a multi-strand item to sit separately – they would work on the necklace featured on page 130, for example. However, they add extra length to the piece so make sure you add on the width of the separators, the crimp beads and small coordinating beads used to join the separator to the clasp when calculating the final length.

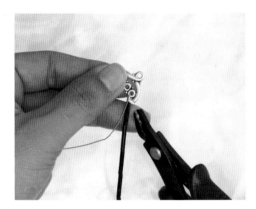

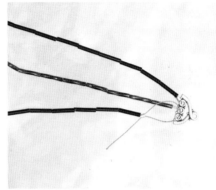

5 Push the crimp bead against the final bead on the strand and push the separator against the crimp bead. Now pull the wire tight. Firmly press the crimp bead to secure the wire using the crimping pliers or needle-nose pliers then trim off the end of the wire.

6 Attach the remaining strands to the separator in the same way, as shown, each time making sure that the crimp bead sits snugly between the separator and the decorative beads on that strand.

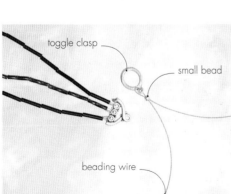

toggle clasp

small bead

beading wire

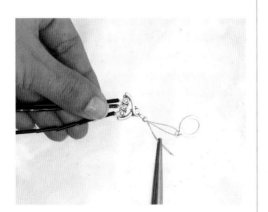

7 Cut a 10cm (4in) length of beading wire and thread on a small bead that matches the clasp or coordinates with the main beads. Slip the wire through the loop on the clasp then pass the wire back through the small bead.

8 Pass both ends of the wire through a crimping bead, through the ring on the separator and back through both beads. Pull the wire tight and crimp (see pages 68–69). Repeat steps 5–8 on the other end.

making rosary loops

Rosary loops are useful for attaching beads to each other, to chains or to the hoop of an ear wire, for example. You can use round-nose pliers for this, as shown, or use rosary pliers, as I do. These have built-in wire cutters for speed and convenience.

tip

An eyepin is like a headpin except that it has a rosary loop in place of the flattened end. If you wish to join several beads together with rosary loops you'll save time by using eyepins instead of headpins.

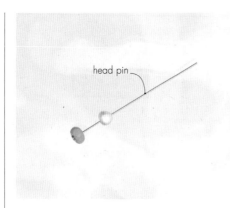

head pin

1 Slide your chosen bead(s) onto a headpin or eyepin in the desired order. You may wish to place a spacer bead between the beads or slide one on first as a decorative detail.

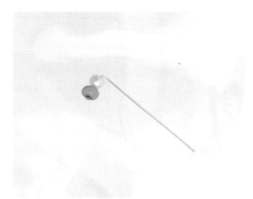

2 Using your index finger from whichever hand feels comfortable, press the wire over at a right angle on top of the upper bead, as shown here.

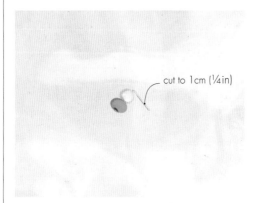

cut to 1cm (¼in)

3 Use wire cutters or the cutters on your rosary pliers to trim the wire extending above the top bead, leaving a length of about 1cm (a little over ¼in).

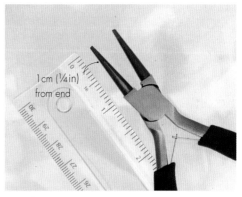

1cm (¼in) from end

4 Find the place on your pliers about 1cm (a little over ¼in) from the end, which is where you'll be wrapping the wire. (The closer you work to the end of the pliers the smaller the loop will be; to start with you'll find larger loops easier to make.)

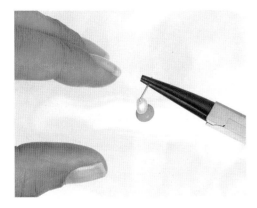

tip

A rosary loop is a quick and easy alternative to a wrapped loop (see pages 78–81). Although it is not as secure as a wrapped loop it has the advantage of using less wire, so if you find you have insufficient wire to make a wrapped loop then just make one of these instead.

5 Use your pliers to grab the very end of the wire at the point 1 cm (¼in) from the tip of the pliers. To ensure even-sized loops on all the beads you must use this position each time.

6 Turn your wrist to curl the wire toward yourself to make a loop. Release the wire and grab it again about halfway along. Curl the wire again.

7 The second twist of the wire should have completed a circle. If not, twist a little more until you have a full loop, as shown. To make larger loops you will need a little more wire remaining in step 3 and to make smaller ones you'll need less wire. With practice you will be able to produce the right combination with ease.

8 Examine the loop to check that the circle is closed, otherwise there is a danger of losing the beads later. Your loop should look like the one shown on the right. To attach the rosary loop to another loop, lift the end slightly. Do not push the loop open from inside or you will distort it and it will not go back into shape.

wire wrapping

Wire wrapping creates a sturdy loop on the end of a bead or series of beads that have been strung on wire, headpins or eyepins. This technique is invaluable for making earrings, adding drops to a necklace or bracelet or for any other project with wired elements.

you will need

tools

Needle-nose or chain-nose pliers

Round-nose or rosary pliers

Wire cutters

materials

Wire, headpin or eyepin

Beads for your chosen project

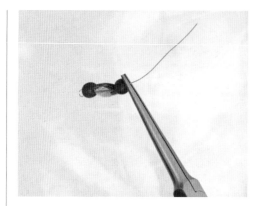

1 Place your chosen bead(s) on the wire, headpin or eyepin, making sure they go all the way down the shaft. You will need 15–25mm (½–1in) of wire protruding above the top bead to complete the wrap. (It is easier with longer wire, but also more wasteful.)

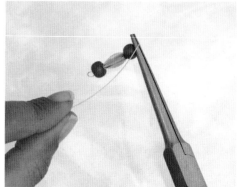

2 Grab the wire just above the beads with the tips of your needle-nose pliers. Take care when using crystal or semi-precious beads that the pliers don't damage them. Pull the wire over the pliers at a right angle, as shown, to create a shank for the wire wrapping.

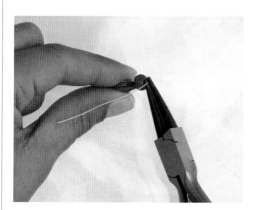

3 Grasp the bent wire with your round-nose pliers just beyond the bend, as shown. The closer you are to the end of the pliers, the smaller the final loop will be.

4 Use your free hand to pull the end of the wire over the tip of the pliers, as shown, taking it tightly around the pliers to begin the loop that will be attached to the next element of the jewellery, such as an ear wire.

tip

As you become more proficient at wire wrapping you will develop your own version of the technique. To create a tight wrap around the stem of the wire in step 8 some people find it helpful to use needle-nose pliers so that you can pull tight as you wrap.

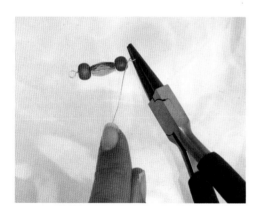

5 Pull the wire around as far as it will go in a smooth movement to create a neat loop. With a little practice you will be able to do this quickly and neatly. You have completed three-quarters of the loop.

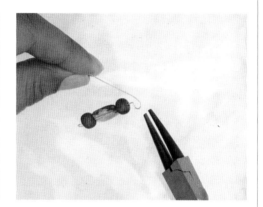

6 This is what the loop looks like. At this point you can slip another component into the open loop, such as an ear wire, chain link or rosary loop. I haven't done this because I want the process to be easy for you to see.

7 Slip the round-nose pliers back in the loop and grasp the end of the wire with your free hand. Wrap it around the pliers to complete the loop and bring you to the starting position for the wrapping.

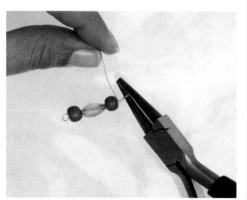

8 Wrap the wire twice around the stem below the loop (see the tip, top left). The end of the wire should finish very close to the bead, as shown. Snip off the end of the wire close to the bead so that the end is barely seen.

making a double wrap

If you can wire wrap as explained on the previous pages, then it is a simple matter to repeat the process at both ends of a bead or set of beads, making a double wrap. You'll need this technique for the drop necklace on page 142 and for the rope necklace on page 146.

you will need

tools

Needle-nose or chain-nose pliers

Round-nose or rosary pliers

Wire cutters

materials

Headpin or wire

Bead(s) suitable for the project

Items to attach, in this case a clasp and chain

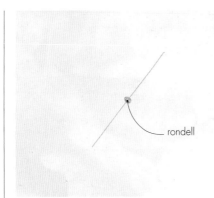

rondell

1 Slip the bead you are using, here a gold corrugated rondell, onto a short length of wire and trim the wire so that you have 15–25mm (½–1in) extending above and below the bead. Alternatively use a long headpin.

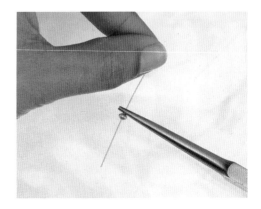

2 Grasp the wire just above the bead with your needle-nose or chain-nose pliers, as shown, and pull the wire over at a right angle. If you wish you can slip off the bead at this point but I have left it in place so that you can see how the technique progresses.

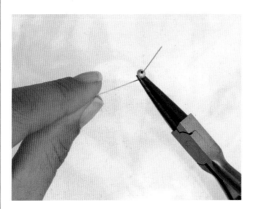

3 Switch to the round-nose pliers and grab the bent portion of the wire exactly at the bend. Use your free hand to take the wire around the pliers, making a loop (see steps 3–5 on pages 78–79).

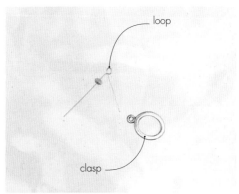

loop

clasp

4 Slip one of the two components you wish to join together into the loop of the wire. In this case it is going to be part of a toggle clasp.

tip

If your wire wrapping isn't as neat as you'd like it to be, use a bead that matches the colour of your wire rather than the main bead colour in the jewellery. A contrasting bead will draw attention to itself – and the wrapping – whereas a matching bead will melt into the background.

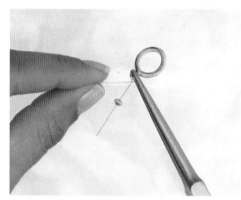

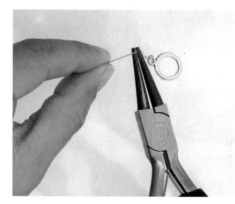

5 Complete the wire wrap by wrapping the end of the wire around the stem just below the loop in the usual way, following steps 7–8 on page 79.

6 If you slipped off the bead in step 2, you need to thread it back on now. Grasp the wire just above the bead with your needle-nose pliers and bend the wire over at a right angle. Change to your round-nose pliers, as shown, and make another loop, as before.

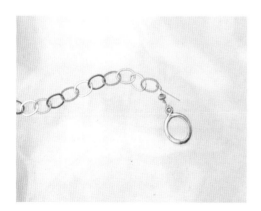

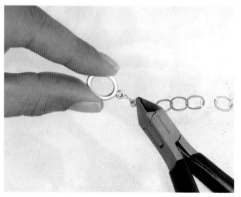

7 Slip on the other component, in this case the gold chain of a necklace, and then complete the wire wrap by taking the end of the wire twice around the wire below the loop, finishing close to the bead(s).

8 Use your wire cutters to trim off the end of the wire close to the bead. If the wire end shows, use needle-nose pliers to squeeze it down against the bead where it is out of sight.

wrapping a briolette

Briolettes and other drop beads have a hole running through the top so that when strung they will dangle down. If you need to wire wrap them, you can't use the standard technique. The following method for wire wrapping a briolette gives a gorgeous and sturdy finish.

you will need

tools

Wire cutters

Needle-nose or chain-nose pliers

Rosary or round-nose pliers

materials

Briolette or other bead drop

Soft Flex or equivalent beading wire

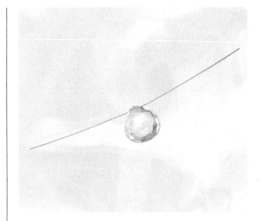

1 Slip a briolette onto a piece of beading wire, leaving about 4cm (1½in) extending on one side and at least 2cm (¾in) on the other side. To start with you may find it helpful to begin with the bead in the centre.

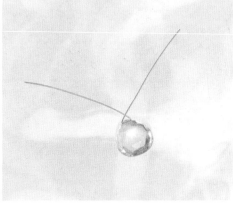

2 Pull the wires across the top of the bead in a cross to form a triangle with the briolette centred inside it, as shown.

3 Use the needle-nose pliers to bend each wire up at the point where the two wires cross, as shown here.

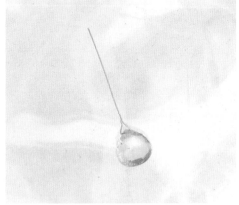

4 Trim off the short end of wire 3mm (⅛in) above the top of the wire triangle using wire cutters. The short end of wire will be covered by the wrap later on.

tip

It's tempting to buy economy materials to practise your techniques with. Unfortunately cheap wire is usually thick and rather stiff and it is very difficult to produce attractive wraps using it. So buy the best wire – you're worth it!

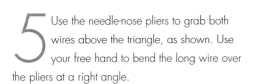

both wires held

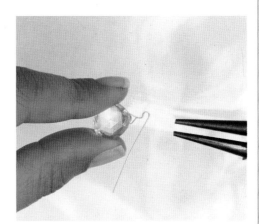

5 Use the needle-nose pliers to grab both wires above the triangle, as shown. Use your free hand to bend the long wire over the pliers at a right angle.

6 Switch to your round-nose pliers and make a loop in the usual way (see steps 3–6 for wire wrapping on pages 78–79). Slip the next component, such as an ear wire, onto the loop, if desired.

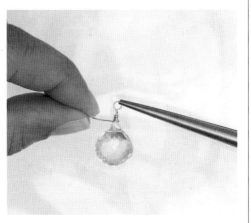

7 Complete the loop by grasping it with the round-nose pliers and taking the wire on round with your free hand.

8 Starting at the base of the loop, wrap the wire around the neck of the wire, keeping the wraps close together. Work on down to the bead then trim the excess wire.

designer projects

earrings

We've worn earrings since at least 2,500 BCE and vase paintings, coins and the like inform us that they were sported by the Ancient Greeks and Egyptians – Tutankhamen had pierced ears. Since then they've been worn by important people everywhere, including Elizabeth I and Queen Victoria of England, and probably by thousands of lesser known, less wealthy people too; so think of your earring designs as forwarding a long-established line. And because earrings are some of the quickest, easiest and most wearable jewellery items around, there are plenty of reasons to get started.

all about earrings

Earrings are usually the first project people attempt to make. They require the least amount of beads and findings, and some of the simplest designs can be completed in a matter of minutes. With that said, there are also complicated earring designs that can take hours to make.

There are a wide variety of earring shapes and designs. While there used to be strict rules for the wearing of certain styles, people no longer worry about these conventions. Although items such as elaborate diamond earrings are mostly reserved for evening wear, nearly all other shapes and styles can be worn with any fashion, casual or formal, night or day.

basic styles

Chandeliers utilize components, chain and other mechanisms that add dimension and length.

Dangles hang down seductively from the ear. These can be made with a single bead or with many depending on the look you're trying to achieve.

Hoops are circular or semi-circular wires that look like a ring. They go through the ear front to back in a loop or can be attached to ear wires (see pages 160–161).

Posts & studs are straight wires that go through the ear and are secured on the back with a small component called a clutch, butterfly clip or earnut.

shapes for different faces

Experiment with different shapes and styles of earrings to see the way they change the look of your face.

• Oval faces work with any shape of earring, though the earrings should be balanced to the size of the wearer.

• A round face needs earrings with length to elongate it. A drop earring works best.

• An oblong face looks good with a button earring, drawing the eye horizontally.

• A heart-shaped face needs earrings that are wider at the bottom to balance a narrow chin. Shapes such as teardrops and inverted triangles work particularly well but button earrings can also be flattering.

• A diamond-shaped face can follow the same "rules" as an oval but this face shape can also carry a more dramatic design. Corners, points and harder edges complement the angular face; cut crystals are especially nice with the diamond-shaped face.

• For a square-shaped face try drop earrings, which add flattering length.

endless hoops
If you have an oval or diamond-shaped face you can carry off these lovely hoops (page 92).

pearls with everything
Pearls go with just about
everything and anything, which
is why they are so enduringly
popular. These clusters are ideal
for square, round and heart-
shaped faces (see pages 98–99).

earring projects

There are six lovely earrings to make
in this section, none of which should
be too difficult, even for the relatively
inexperienced, and you'll find more
easy examples in the Quick & Easy
section on pages 158–165. Projects
marked with one bead are suitable
for beginners; two for intermediates.

bead drop

●○○　90–91

circle of life

●○○　92–93

multi-drop

●●○　94–95

swing-time

●●○　96–97

pearl clusters

●○○　98–99

snowdrop hoops

●○○　100–101

bead drop earrings

Elegant in their simplicity, these easy-to-wear earrings can be made in a matter of minutes yet provide a lifetime of pleasure. You only need two beads for each one, so you can afford to buy the best – these are made in a stunning combination of turquoise and freshwater pearls.

you will need

tools

Wire cutters

Needle-nose or chain-nose pliers

Round-nose pliers or rosary pliers

materials

4 beads of your choice – I used 2 x 4mm pearls and 2 x 4mm turquoise rondells

2 gold-colour headpins

4 gold-colour daisy spacers

2 gold-colour fishhook ear wires

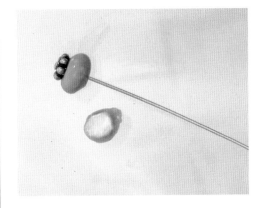

1 Thread a daisy spacer onto one headpin – this not only looks decorative but prevents beads with large holes falling off the end. Thread on a turquoise rondell.

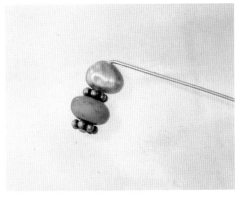

2 Thread on another daisy spacer and then a pearl. Grasp the headpin wire above the top bead firmly with your needle-nose pliers. Using your free hand, bend the headpin over at a right angle.

3 Change to the round-nose pliers and make a wrapped loop following the instructions on pages 78–79. Clip off the excess wire then use the needle-nose pliers to squeeze the wire end close to the beads where it will be almost invisible.

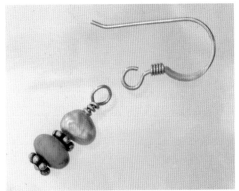

4 Open the ring in the ear wire by pulling it gently with your needle-nose pliers. Insert the loop on the beaded headpin. Close the loop to complete one earring then make the second earring in the same way.

circle of life hoops

Plain hoop earrings are widely available from jewellery stores and make a great basis for some decorative beadwork. You can't slip the beads straight onto them because they are too thick but you can wrap them with fine wire, adding the beads of your choice to create a unique piece in no time.

you will need

tools

Wire cutters

Needle-nose or chain-nose pliers

materials

40mm (1½in) plain endless hoops in silver, available from jewellery stores

50cm (20in) of 26-gauge wire in silver

32 small beads – I used 4mm blue quartz and 3mm silver beads

2 large centre drops – mine were 12mm aquamarine briolettes

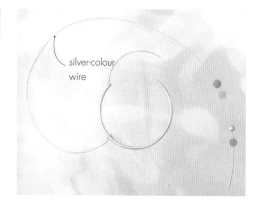

silver-colour wire

1 Cut a 25cm (10in) length of silver-colour wire. Starting about ¼ of the way down from the top of the hoop, wrap the wire tightly around the hoop, locking it in place. Slide three or four beads onto the wire.

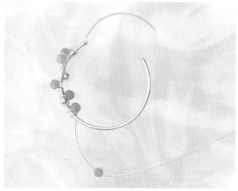

2 Wrap the wire around the hoop so that the beads fit tightly against it. For a snug fit, hold the hoop and pull the wire gently with needle-nose pliers. Repeat the process with three or four more beads.

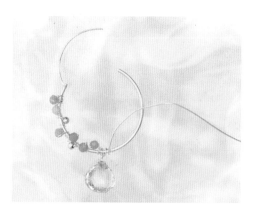

3 When you reach the bottom of the hoop you can add the briolette. Wire wrap it following the instructions on pages 82–83 then slip the briolette onto the wire. Take the wire to the other side of the briolette by wrapping it.

4 Wrap the second side of the hoop as before, sliding on three or four beads at a time and pulling tight. Finally, wrap wire around the hoop as at the beginning. Weave the wire back through the last group of beads and trim off the excess. Repeat to make a second earring.

multi-drop earrings

Designed for impact, these earrings are real attention grabbers and make great party wear. They are hugely adaptable, and you can have lots of fun experimenting with different bead shapes and sizes. Try other colours too, to suit your personal taste or a particular outfit.

you will need

tools

Wire cutters

Narrow-nose or chain-nose pliers

Round-nose or rosary pliers

materials

Selection of beads – I used 2 wooden disc beads 8mm across; 2 round translucent pink beads 8mm across; 4 round translucent pink beads 6mm across; 26 purple beads 3mm across; 2 small round gold beads, and a handful of fire-polished pink seed beads

2 gold fishhook ear wires

8 gold-colour headpins

8 gold-colour daisy spacers

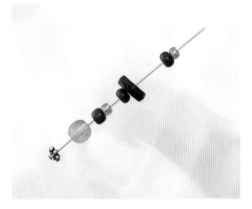

1 Thread your chosen beads onto the first headpin. I started with a daisy spacer, then added a 6mm pink bead, three pink and purple beads, the wooden disc and then two more pink and purple beads.

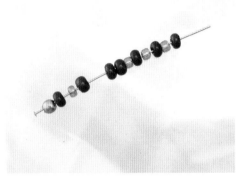

2 Thread beads onto the second headpin. Here I created a narrow column, starting with a gold bead and then adding an arrangement of small pink and purple beads.

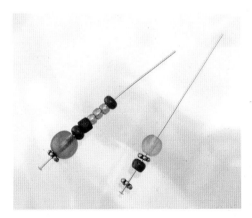

3 Thread beads onto the third and fourth headpins. Aim for variety in length and width and remember that you need to save an equal quantity of beads to make the second, matching earring.

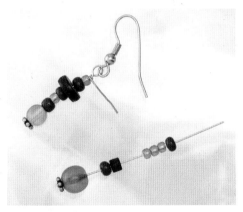

4 Referring to the instructions on pages 78–79, make a wrapped loop at the top of each headpin and slip it onto the ear wire. Repeat to make the second earring.

swing-time earrings

This chandelier style is elegant and sophisticated, and these lovely earrings are perfect for a special dinner or evening at the theatre. They could also be adapted to coordinate with bridal wear. Make them in shades of a single colour or in two or three linking colours.

you will need

tools

Wire cutters

Needle-nose or chain-nose pliers

Round-nose or rosary pliers

Crimping pliers

materials

2 briolettes 20mm long – mine were smoky quartz

10 small watermelon tourmalines about 3mm across

20cm (8in) length of gold-colour chain

20cm (8in) length of Soft Flex beading wire or equivalent

2 gold-colour fishhook ear wires

4 gold-colour spacer beads

4 gold-colour crimp beads

2 gold-colour headpins

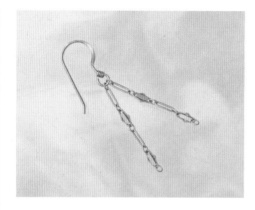

1 Open the loop on the ear wire by pulling sideways. Cut two 40mm (1½in) chains and slip them onto the ear wire to check they are the same. If your chain only has one type of link, you can use a single 80mm (3in) length.

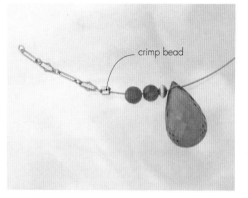

crimp bead

2 Take the chain off the ear wire. Cut a 10cm (4in) length of beading wire and crimp one side to the end of one chain as explained on pages 68–69. Add two tourmaline beads, a gold spacer and then the centre drop.

3 Now add a second gold spacer and then two more tourmaline beads. Add a second crimp bead. If you have two short chains, crimp the beaded wire to the other chain. If you have one longer chain, crimp the beaded wire to the free end.

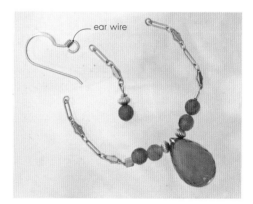

ear wire

4 For the centre dangle, cut a 12mm (½in) length of chain. Take a headpin and thread on a bead and a gold spacer then wire wrap it to the end of the chain as explained on pages 78–79. Slip the chains on the ear wire and close the loop. Repeat for the second earring.

pearl clusters

Pearls have always been associated with elegance, sophistication and purity, and for this reason are often chosen for bridal wear, although they are suitable for any formal event. These pearl cluster earrings are very quick to make and easily adapted using other beads.

you will need

tools

Needle-nose or chain-nose pliers

Thread snips or scissors

materials

12 pearl beads about 8mm across

40cm (16in) of clear nylon beading thread

2 gold-colour daisy spacers

2 small gold crimp beads

2 gold-colour fishhook ear wires

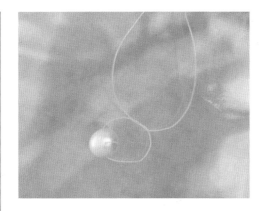

1 Cut 20cm (8in) of beading thread and slide one bead to the centre. Tie a simple overhand knot with the two ends of thread, enclosing the bead, as shown.

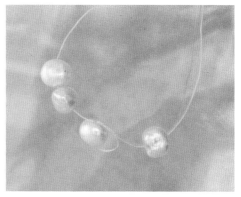

2 Tighten the knot in the thread. Now slide two beads on one end of the thread and one bead on the other end, as shown. Tighten up the thread again. This time the extra beads will help to keep the knot in place.

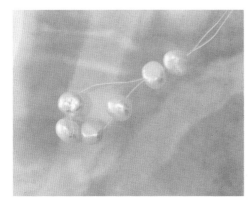

3 Take both ends of beading thread together and slide on two more pearl beads, as shown. Push the beads down the thread until they sit tightly against the beads already in place.

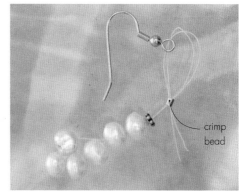

crimp bead

4 Thread on a daisy spacer then a crimp bead. Push the thread through the eye on an ear wire and then back through the crimp bead. Pull the thread tight, crimp the bead and trim the thread (see pages 68–69). Repeat for the second earring.

snowdrop hoops

Metal hoops like these come in a variety of sizes in either gold or silver colours and adding the beads couldn't be simpler. If you want to completely cover the hoops in beads, as here, you'll need to incorporate some small ones, such as seed beads, to ensure a good fit.

you will need

tools

Needle-nose or chain-nose pliers

materials

2 x 30mm (1¼in) silver hoops with ear wires

Handful of clear seed beads

4 mother-of-pearl chips

4 large silver-coloured daisy spacers

2 large clear focal beads – mine were 10mm

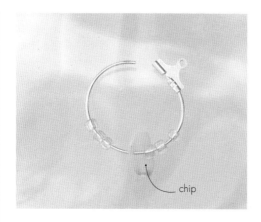

chip

daisy spacer

1 Beads are threaded on from one end of the hoop and to get a balanced effect you may need to make a few adjustments. For this design start by threading on three seed beads, a chip and then another three seed beads.

2 Thread on a large silver daisy spacer, your focal bead and then another daisy spacer. The focal bead should sit opposite the end with the ring. If not you may need to adjust the number of seed beads on the hoop.

ear wire

3 Thread on three seed beads, a mother-of-pearl chip and then another three seed beads, as shown. The hoop should now be nearly full but with just enough wire left at the end to slip into the fitting easily.

4 Push the loose hoop end into the fitting, check the effect and when you are happy with it squeeze the fitting with your pliers. Add the ear wire to complete your first earring then make the other one to match.

bracelets

Worn by both men and women since we first started metalworking, bracelets began as a symbol of wealth and status. Egyptian kings and Roman governors were weighed down with them – coiled metal serpents (a little like memory wire bracelets today), ornate armbands and plenty of bangles, sometimes encrusted with jewels. Today's beaded bracelets can be whatever you want them to be, from the frivolous and feminine to chunky, masculine or even functional (medical bracelets). By making one yourself you can be sure to create exactly the right look for you.

all about bracelets

The term bracelet usually refers to a flexible piece of jewellery that drapes softly around the wrist. There are many different styles of bracelets and lots of materials to choose from. A beaded bracelet is strung with stones or beads and can be a single strand, double, triple or as many strands as you want to make.

A well-fitting bracelet should be loose enough to be comfortable and not put pressure on your wrist, yet snug enough so it does not slide too far down onto your hand or even fall off. An average size bracelet is 18cm (7in) long. I usually make mine 18.5cm (7¼in) for extra wiggle room but make yours to fit your wrists.

basic styles

Bangles are metal circles that fit over the wrist. They are usually narrow and are often worn in pairs or trios for a stacked look. A bangle may be an endless circle hinged so that it is easier to put on. A new trend is to add charms and multi-coloured stones for a bohemian look.

Cuffs are solid bracelets, often inflexible, that do not circle the entire wrist and tend to be wider than bangles. A cuff can be made purely of metal, wood or plastic, or it can be mixed with gemstones for added luxury.

Charm bracelets are usually linked chain adorned with tiny sentimental pendants. I also like to add bead dangles from the links (see pages 116–117).

bracelet lengths

Measure the intended wrist, leaving a little slack for a comfortable fit. Subtract the length of the clasp and ring assembly. The result is the desired length of beading for your bracelet. However, large beads take up more space and could make it too tight. To assure that a finished bracelet will fit correctly you need to compensate for the diameter of your beads. For round beads, add three beads to the measured length of your strand. For any other shape, triple the diameter of one bead and add enough beads to your strand to make up that additional length. Before you add the clasp, hold the bracelet up to your wrist to ensure it fits properly.

thick and thin
Combine beads of different sizes in one or two colours for a classic look. (See pages 112–115 for detailed instructions on making this bracelet.)

the more the merrier
If you can make a single-strand bracelet then a multi-strand version will be no problem. This bracelet features on page 108.

bracelet projects

These four bracelets are so lovely you'll probably want to make them all, and before you know it you will have mastered most of the techniques in this book. The first project (marked with a single bead) is for beginners, the next two are intermediate and the final project is more advanced.

eye of the tiger

●○○ 106–107

lucky green

●●○ 108–111

vintage multi-strand

●●○ 112–115

metal magic

●●● 116–117

eye of the tiger

Combining different types of beads in a single colour is an easy way to ensure that the piece has variety and interest while maintaining an overall harmony. This piece combines semi-precious stones with wood for an earthy combination that goes with most styles.

you will need

tools

Wire cutters
Crimping pliers

materials

30cm (12in) length of Soft Flex beading wire or equivalent

10 faceted tiger's eye beads 6mm long

4 oval wood beads 8mm long

4 faceted nugget citrine beads about 18mm long

17 gold-colour spacer beads

2 gold-colour crimp beads

1 gold-colour toggle clasp 10mm long

Transparent sticky tape

1 Stick a piece of tape to the beading wire about 5cm (2in) from one end to prevent the beads falling off. Thread on a spacer and tiger's eye bead twice then add a wooden oval, as shown.

2 Thread on another spacer followed by one of the focal beads – a citrine nugget. Now repeat steps 1 and 2 to build up the pattern or create a symmetrical pattern around the citrines as I did in my finished piece.

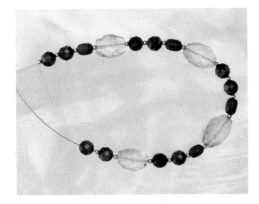

3 Continue stringing until you reach the desired length – I favour 18.5cm (7¼in) including the clasp. In order to create the required length I left off one oval bead before the clasp, which will be unnoticeable once the bracelet is complete.

toggle clasp

4 Add a crimp bead and crimp the end of the beading wire to the toggle clasp, following the instructions on pages 68– 69. Remove the tape from the loose end of the wire, slip on the other crimp bead and crimp that end to the free end of the clasp to finish.

lucky green bracelet

Why settle for one strand of beads when four is so much more fun? This charming multi-strand bracelet is as easy to make as a single-strand bracelet and the unique combination of rectangular beads, round crystals and tiny silver charms make this bracelet a bohemian girl's dream.

you will need

tools

Wire cutters
Crimping pliers

materials

Soft Flex beading wire or equivalent

2 x 40cm (16in) long strands of irregular rectangular beads, each about 6–10mm long (I used malachite)

About 12 round clear glass, crystal or acrylic beads 5mm across

Roughly 10 or more silver charms

4-strand silver clasp

8 silver crimp beads

Transparent sticky tape

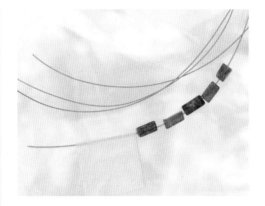

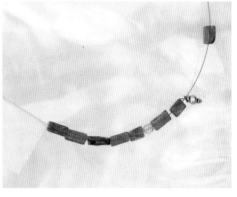

1 Decide on the total length of your bracelet (see page 104) and deduct the length of the clasp to find the finished length of each strand. Cut four equal lengths of beading wire to your calculated measurement plus 10cm (4in) or more. Stick some tape over one wire about 5cm (2in) from the end and start stringing.

2 Space the crystal beads and charms as desired. You may wish to add the charms to just one of the strands or add two or three to each strand, and you may like to add the crystal or acrylic beads at regular intervals or work randomly, as I did.

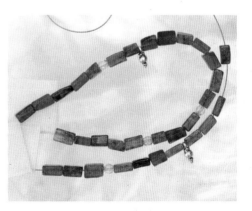

3 Thread on more beads to complete one strand, remembering that you have four strands to fill – don't use up all your most decorative beads on the first one.

4 Stick tape over the end of the second strand and begin stringing on the beads. At intervals lay your strand beside the first one to check they work well together.

If you like multi-strand bracelets and necklaces then look out for a multi-strand beading board (see pages 64–65). These have parallel channels in which you can place your strands to compare them. The strands won't roll around, the beads won't fall off, and if you are using semi-precious stones as I do, it will help to protect them from being scratched or broken.

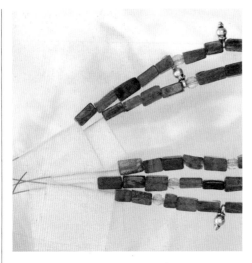

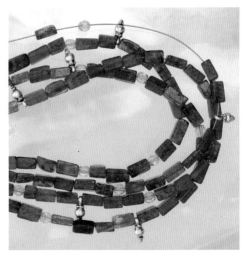

5 String up the third strand in exactly the same way, laying it alongside the other two strands at intervals to check that the appearance is balanced.

6 Now you can string up your fourth and final strand in exactly the same way. When complete, lay out all the strands together and make a final check to be sure you are happy with the bead arrangements. This is your last chance to make any adjustments.

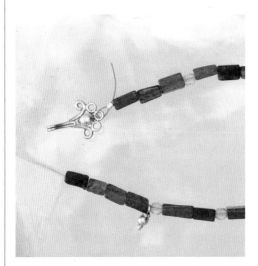

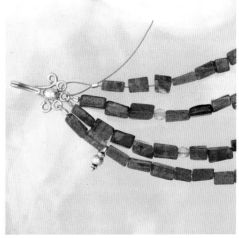

7 The clasp I chose was designed for five strands, not four, so I am going to attach two strands to the centre loop and one on each side, leaving the outer loops empty. If you have a four-strand clasp, use all four loops. Remove the tape from the end of the first strand you are going to attach and use a crimp bead to attach it to a loop in the clasp (see pages 68–69).

8 Use the crimping technique to attach the remaining strands to the clasp, as shown. Attach the other ends of the strands to the other part of the clasp in the same way, making sure that the strands are not twisted and lie parallel to each other. There, you've done it!

all change

Green not your favourite colour? There's no need to copy my design exactly – use any stones of your choice. If you wish to use bulkier beads, try three strands instead of four, and if one colour isn't to your taste, combine two or more as in the amethyst bracelet on the right, which makes use of wood, metal and amethyst.

large amethyst beads add class and provide a focus

dyed wooden beads are a link between the amethysts and the plain wooden beads

carnelian chips are inexpensive, yet look as if they cost a fortune

wooden beads suit many occasions

metal leaf charms emphasize the natural theme

vintage multi-strand

This triple-strand bracelet is glamorous yet subtle enough to wear on a host of different occasions – it's bound to become a treasured favourite. It's made in the classic combination of gold and black, but there are plenty of alternatives, limited only by your imagination (see page 115).

(see page 115)

you will need

tools

Wire cutters

Needle-nose or chain-nose pliers

Crimping pliers

Tape measure

materials

About 9 black round glass beads 8–10mm long

About 8 bicone beads 18mm long

Pinch of seed beads

1 gold-plated triple-strand clasp

18 gold-plated bead ends to fit the round glass beads

6 gold-plated crimp beads

Soft Flex beading wire or equivalent

Transparent sticky tape

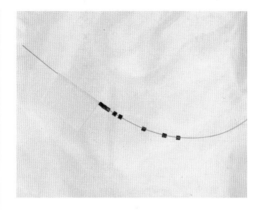

1 Decide on the length of your bracelet and deduct the length of the clasp. Cut three 30cm (12in) lengths of beading wire and begin your first strand by folding a piece of tape over the stringing wire 5cm (2in) from the end. String on a few seed beads.

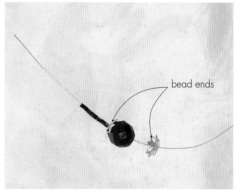

bead ends

2 Continue applying the beads. I added a round glass bead next, with a gold-plated bead end on each side, as shown. The bead ends draw attention to the beads and add a luxurious touch, which I like.

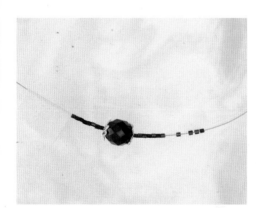

3 Add some more seed beads – the number you use depends on the size of the beads and personal preference.

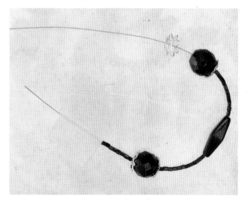

4 Continue to build up the pattern. I added a bicone bead next followed by some more seed beads and then another round glass bead, remembering to add the bead ends on each end, as before.

5 Continue the stringing process until the first strand is the desired length. I added some more seed beads, another bicone bead and then a final group of seed beads. You can string up the beads in a different order but make sure you start and finish with seed beads. Attach a piece of tape to the end of the wire.

6 String up a second strand in the same way. Begin and end with a different number of seed beads and change the order of the large beads to create a staggered look when compared with the first strand. Check that both strands are the same length then stick tape to the end of the wire.

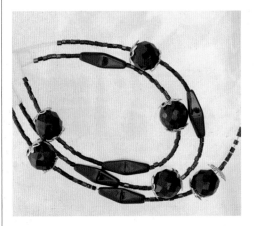

7 Now string up the third and final strand, again starting and finishing with seed beads. Aim to position the large beads so that when all three strands are placed together there are no obvious gaps. As before, make sure you apply a piece of tape to the ends of the wire to prevent the beads falling off.

8 Each beaded strand goes through its own hole on the triple-strand clasp. Attach the strands to the main part of the clasp one by one following the instructions for crimping on pages 68–69. Close the clasp then attach the beaded strands to the other section of the clasp in the same order – top strand to top hole, centre strand to centre hole and so on. Make sure that the strands are not twisted. You have now produced a multi-strand bracelet to treasure.

fit for a princess

When you're in a frivolous mood, the elegant combination of black and gold may not fit the bill. Here amethyst crystal beads combine with gold for a princess look, while a variation in turquoise is more bohemian.

ceramic beads add colour and pattern

seed beads provide a change of pace

fire-polished rondells shimmer in the light

bead ends are an inexpensive means of adding glamour

smaller, paler crystal beads sparkle like precious gems

crystal catches the light like nothing else

metal magic

This bracelet is all about contrasts – heavy beads on a lightweight chain; muted gold tones with shiny silver. It's made with plated beads and chain but can be re-created in precious metals for added elegance or in glass, crystal or acrylic drop beads for colour.

you will need

tools

Wire cutters

Needle-nose or chain-nose pliers

Round-nose or rosary pliers

materials

16½cm (6½in) length of gold-colour chain, available from jewellers

Silver-plated oval beads about 10mm long – I used 26

Small gold-colour seed beads – I used 26

Gold-colour headpins in a long, fine size to match the number of beads

4 more headpins or fine gold-colour wire

2 small gold beads

1 toggle clasp

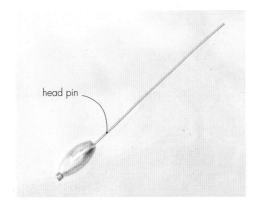

head pin

1 Slide a small gold-colour seed bead onto a long headpin and then slide on one of your oval beads. The gold seed bead adds a decorative touch and prevents the oval bead falling off the end.

2 Wire wrap the headpin to the second or third link in the chain following the instructions on pages 78–79. Take time to do this neatly because your workmanship will be highly visible in the finished piece.

3 Wire wrap further beaded headpins at intervals along the length of chain. This chain has large links alternating with small links and I attached the beads to every small link. Aim to attach them to the same side of a link each time or on alternating sides.

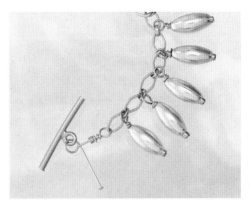

4 Attach the chain to the clasp at each end by double wrapping with a small gold bead (see pages 80–81). You can use headpins for this but otherwise you'll need a little bit of gold-colour wire. You are finished and ready to sparkle in your new bracelet.

necklaces

Necklaces have been used through history for ornamental purposes and to indicate rank or status – in the Bible we learn that a gold chain was part of Joseph's investiture in Egypt. As some of the largest and most obviously displayed items of jewellery, necklaces have huge impact, but that doesn't mean they have to be complicated to make. Indeed, their size means that they are often less tricky than smaller bracelets or earrings, and since the clasp is hidden at the back of the neck or under long hair, you don't need to be dexterous to produce an item of great beauty and desirability.

all about necklaces

A necklace is any piece of jewellery that wraps around the neck, ranging from collar to lariat. There are chunky styles and dainty drops, multi-strands and single strings, elegant pieces and ethnic ones. In fact, it can be difficult to decide what to make first given the overwhelming choice.

Most necklaces comprise a string or strings of beads with a single clasp at the end, though there are exceptions: if the necklace is long enough there may be no need for a clasp, or you can make one long string, called a lariat (see below). Here are some of the basic options.

necklace categories

Collars (30–33cm/12–13in) are usually made up of multiple strands that lie snugly on the middle of the neck. The style is reminiscent of the Victorian age and goes best with V-neck, boat-neck and off-the-shoulder styles.

Chokers (35–40cm/14–16in) are considered the classic-length necklaces and the most versatile of all the single-strand lengths. They sit right above the collarbone and can therefore be worn with just about any neckline imaginable. When I first started making jewellery, all my necklaces were chokers.

Princess necklaces (43–49cm/17–19in) are a very popular medium length and ideally suited for a range of necklines from crew to plunging. They are also the perfect support for a pendant.

Matinee necklaces (50–60cm/20–24in) are longer than princess length. They are commonly worn with casual and business attire.

Opera-length necklaces (70–86cm/28–30in) are the queens of necklaces. When worn as a single strand they have a sophisticated look and they are perfect for high or crew necklines. When doubled they can covert to elegant two-strand chokers.

Rope or lariat lengths (115cm/45in or more) are the longest of all. Ropes can have clasps placed in strategic locations enabling them to convert into multi-strand necklace and bracelet combinations. Alternatively they may not need a clasp at all. Lariats are long, unjoined strings with no clasp. You can wear one in several ways but it is often doubled around the neck and then the ends passed through the loop and pulled down. It can also be knotted at the front (see page 126).

long and luscious
This rope-length necklace can be worn long or doubled or even tripled (see pages 146–149).

pendant power
A stunning shell pendant gives weight to this lovely matinee-length necklace (see pages 150–153).

necklace projects

Here are eight gorgeous necklaces, all very different. Which one will you choose?

purple reigns

●○○ 122–125

lovely lariat

●○○ 126–129

natural woman

●○○ 130–133

fiesta necklace

●●○ 134–137

pearls with a twist

●●○ 138–141

golden glow

●●○ 142–145

water world

●●● 146–149

island dream

●●○ 150–153

purple reigns

Built around a single colour theme, this necklace is quick to make and easy to wear. It is choker length at 40cm (16in) and uses a stunning mix of amethyst and purple jade. Use your favourite colour for your version in any combination of glass, crystal, acrylic or semi-precious beads.

you will need

tools

Wire cutters
Crimping pliers

materials

51cm (20in) length of Soft Flex beading wire or equivalent

20 faceted amethyst beads 4mm long

10 x 18mm smooth oval amethyst beads

27 smooth briolette drops in purple jade about 12mm long

20 silver daisy spacers

2 silver crimp beads

1 silver hook clasp

Transparent sticky tape

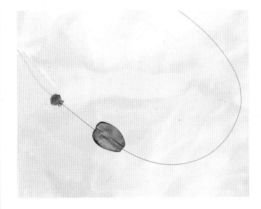

1 Fold a piece of tape about 5cm (2in) from one end of the beading wire to prevent the beads falling off. String on a 4mm faceted bead followed by a daisy spacer and then an oval bead, as shown.

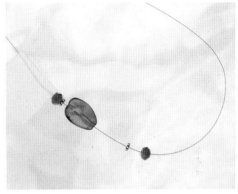

2 Add another daisy spacer followed by a 4mm faceted bead to complete one section of the pattern or work to your own design, if desired.

briolette drop

3 Now add a group of three briolette drops and position them as shown to form a cluster. These will sit snugly in position once the stringing is completed.

4 Repeat steps 1–3 four more times. This takes you to the centre of the necklace. If you are using semi-precious stones, the beads will be variable, so use your best specimens at the centre front.

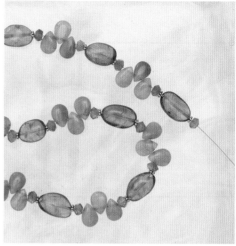

5 Repeat steps 1–3 another four times. As you work your way on from the centre front check that the arrangement is balanced with a symmetrical effect on each side.

6 Now string on a rondell followed by a daisy spacer then an oval bead, a daisy spacer and the final rondell to complete the stringing.

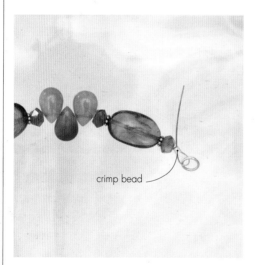

crimp bead

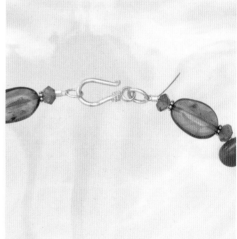

7 Slip on a silver crimp bead and then one part of the clasp. Slip the wire back through the crimp bead and pull tight. Complete the crimping process following the instructions on pages 68–69.

8 Before adding the clasp to the other end of the string, check the length of the necklace by holding it in place at your neck. Close the clasp. Now remove the tape from the end of the wire, add a crimp bead and crimp to the remaining portion of the clasp in the same way as before. You've finished.

night and day

Here are two gorgeous alternatives made in the same way as Purple Reigns. For sheer evening elegance combine smoky quartz with glittering gold; for daytime try a fabulous mix of turquoise and silver, a tried-and-tested combination that always comes out on top.

hurricane glass beads are beautiful yet inexpensive

silver melon beads with daisy spacers at each end work well with the turquoise briolettes

these flat turquoise briolettes are uneven, giving a relaxed, natural look

decorative gold-colour beads add instant glamour

faceted smoky quartz briolettes look sophisticated

lovely lariat

This fun project has a western feel. There's no clasp to worry about so it's quick to complete, and it can be worn in many different ways. This one is made in a daring mix of peach, white and turquoise – do the unexpected and mix up your materials in the same way for beautiful results.

you will need

tools

Wire cutters

Crimping pliers

Beading board or material for laying out beads (optional)

materials

140cm (51in) length of Soft Flex beading wire or equivalent

120cm (47in) of assorted beads – I used coral, turquoise and freshwater pearl

2 pinches of seed beads

50 or so 4–5mm vermeil daisy spacers

2 turquoise focal beads – mine were 8–10mm

2 gold-colour crimp beads

Transparent sticky tape

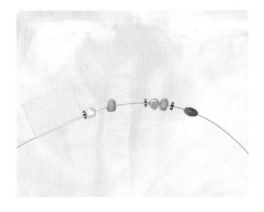

1 Stick a piece of transparent tape about 5cm (2in) from one end of your beading wire to prevent the beads falling off. Start stringing on the beads, either following my design or making up your own. I began with a daisy spacer, white pearl, seed bead, coral, spacer, pink pearl, turquoise, spacer and then coral tube.

2 Once you have strung on a few beads it's time to add a focal bead. I used a large, smooth, oval turquoise bead that picks up the colour of the smaller turquoise beads.

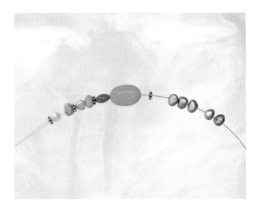

3 The body of the necklace is strung using the different beads in groups for impact. String on one daisy spacer, five black pearls, followed by another daisy spacer.

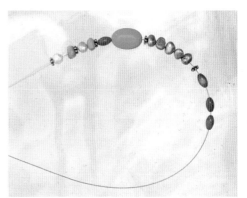

4 Now string on the next batch of beads. I added three coral tubes to link back to the coral at the beginning of the necklace.

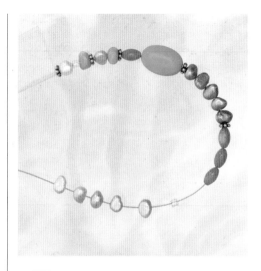

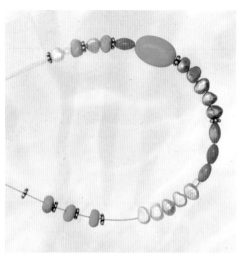

5 Now I added a small clear bead followed by five lovely freshwater pearls in a pale pink colour. Notice how most of the beads – the coral and pearl – can be found under the sea, giving this necklace a lovely theme.

6 Next I added three turquoise rondells, drawing attention to these lovely beads by placing a daisy spacer either side of each one for impact.

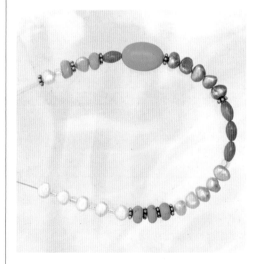

7 This time I combined white freshwater pearls with clear seed beads, using the seed beads as spacers between the pearls, as shown.

8 Continue to add beads in the same way. When you reach halfway – 60cm (23½in) – you may wish to repeat your beading in reverse order for symmetry. Continue until your string is about 120cm (47in) long.

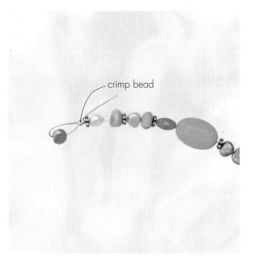

crimp bead

9 Now string on a crimp bead followed by a black pearl. Thread the wire back through the crimp bead, as shown. Tighten the wire so the crimp bead is touching the pearl then use crimping pliers to squeeze the crimp bead flat. Clip off the excess wire close to the crimp bead.

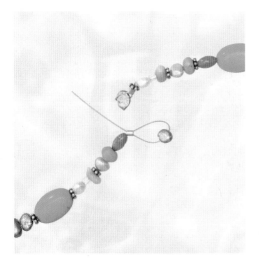

10 Take the tape off the other end of the string and slip on a crimp bead followed by a black pearl. Repeat step 9 to complete the lariat.

mix & match

Change the beads and you get completely different looks – who would have thought these alternatives were made in the same way as the turquoise and coral lariat?

silver balls
add glamour

bright red acrylic
beads add bulk
without much cost

wooden discs
provide a change
of pace

natural woman

Wooden beads come in many lovely colours from cream through buff to mahogany and black, and they have a wonderfully silky surface. Make the most of this variety with a multi-strand necklace that uses a wide selection for an exciting and highly tactile finish.

you will need

tools

Wire cutters

Crimping pliers

materials

230cm (90in) length of Soft Flex beading wire or equivalent

43cm (17in) strand of 4mm pale wood beads

46cm (18in) strand of 5mm rough-cut wood beads

48cm (19in) strand of 6–8mm round carved wood beads

51cm (20in) strand of 15mm flat square beads

Handful of 3mm brown glass beads

9 gold-colour beads 10mm long

8 gold-colour crimp beads of a size suitable for your beading wire

1 large gold-colour toggle clasp

Transparent sticky tape

1 This necklace has four strands, 43cm (17in), 46cm (18in), 48cm (19in), and 51cm (20in). Start by stringing the shortest strand first. To do this cut a 53cm (21in) length of beading wire and fold a piece of tape over it about 5cm (2in) from one end. Start stringing on the 4mm light wood beads.

2 Keep adding the light wood beads until your string is 43cm (17in) long. Add a piece of tape to the end to prevent the beads falling off and set this strand to one side.

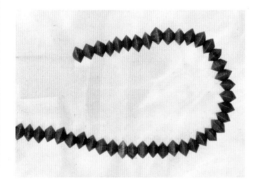

3 Cut a piece of stringing wire 56cm (22in) long and fold a piece of tape over it about 5cm (2in) from one end. Begin stringing the rough-cut wood beads until you have reached 46cm (18in) or the desired length. As before, add a piece of tape and put to one side.

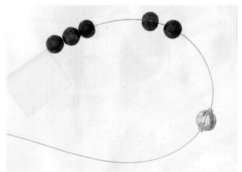

4 Cut a piece of stringing wire 58cm (23in) long and fold a piece of tape over it about 5cm (2in) from one end. Begin stringing the carved wood beads. Add a gold-colour bead after every five wood beads.

tip

I used a simple toggle clasp here for simplicity, but you could try a multi-strand clasp, which will help to keep the strands separate and firmly in position. Another idea is to add a separator just before the clasp (see pages 74–75).

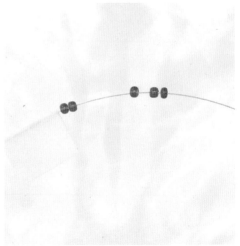

5 Continue to add the beads in the same order until your string is 48cm (19in) long or the desired length. Add a piece of tape to prevent the beads falling off and place the strand aside with the others.

6 Now you are on to your final strand. Cut a fourth piece of stringing wire 61cm (24in) long and fold a piece of tape over it about 5cm (2in) from one end. String on five brown glass beads to start.

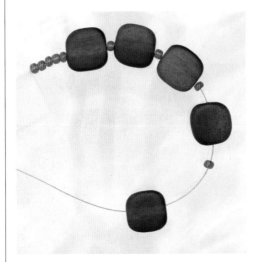

toggle clasp

7 Add a flat square bead followed by a glass bead. Add another square bead, then a glass bead and continue in this way until you have almost reached 51cm (20in) or the desired length. String on five glass beads to finish. Do not attach a piece of tape to the end.

8 Still working with the longest strand, slip on a crimp bead. Thread the wire through the toggle clasp and back through the crimp bead then flatten the crimp bead to secure the strand (see pages 68–69).

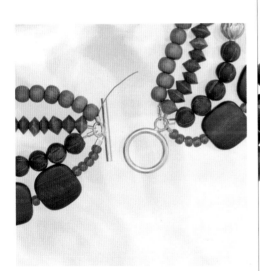

thrifty opportunity

Necklaces like this, which use a variety of beads, provide a great opportunity for using up leftovers, so go through your bead box and see what you can find. Pad out the ones you have with seed beads, glass and metal: you'll be amazed what you can create.

9 Attach the other end of this strand to the second part of the clasp in the same way, making sure the beads are butted up tightly before you crimp.

10 Working from the longest strand to the shortest one, repeat steps 8–9 to attach the remaining strands to the clasp one by one. Make sure the strands are not twisted together. All four strands are now crimped onto one clasp. The necklace should drape layered around your neck.

long metal beads add variety

beads in warm colours make you feel soothed and comforted

faceted yellow glass beads flash in the light to attract attention

seed beads cushion the larger beads, a good idea with semi-precious stones

fiesta necklace

Decked with a glorious combination of dangling briolettes, rondells, round beads and seed beads, this is a colour extravaganza and an excellent way of utilizing any small quantities of beads that you've been saving for that special project. The necklace is princess length at 43–48cm (17–19in).

you will need

tools

Wire cutters

Crimping pliers

Beading board or material for laying out beads (optional)

materials

66cm (26in) length of Soft Flex beading wire or equivalent

20mm centre drop – I used a lemon quartz faceted briolette

Assorted small briolette drops – I used 8mm peridot and blue topaz briolettes, and 5mm aquamarine briolettes

Handful of 2–3mm round beads in blue iolite, aquamarine and green peridot

Handful of 3–5mm rondell beads in garnet, apatite, aquamarine and blue quartz

6 round 8–10mm carnelian beads

Handful of gold-colour seed beads

6 gold-colour spacer beads

2 gold-tone crimp beads

1 gold-colour lobster clasp

1 For necklaces with a centre drop, I like to work my pattern from the middle outward. This way you can match the pattern on each side. You'll be threading from both ends so take care the beads don't slip off. String on the large centre drop to start.

2 This necklace has a random pattern but I was careful to spread out the colours and not place duplicates next to each other. Work out from the centre, placing pairs of beads with one on each side of the centre drop. Create a mix of large, small, and medium beads.

3 Continue to work your way up the sides of the necklace, creating variety in colour and shape. Space distinctive beads, like the reddish carnelians and deep blue topaz beads, at regular intervals.

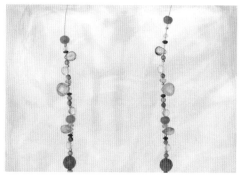

4 Continue in the same way, checking all the time that the effect is symmetrical. Refer to these images and to the main picture if you wish to copy my design exactly.

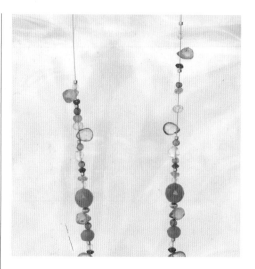

5 Work your way on up the string, aiming for a pleasing, seemingly random selection of beads and mixing briolettes with round beads. Regularly check that both sides are the same – it's only too easy to miss a bead.

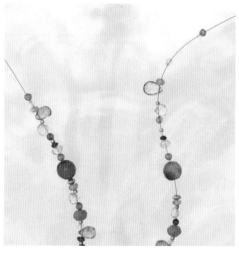

6 You are nearly there. Check the length of the necklace before adding the final beads – my version was 55cm (22in).

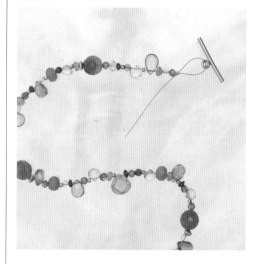

7 Once you have reached the end slip on a gold-colour crimp bead. Thread the wire through the loop on the toggle clasp and back through the crimp bead. Pull the wire up tight and then press the crimp bead with your crimping pliers to secure the strand (see pages 68–69).

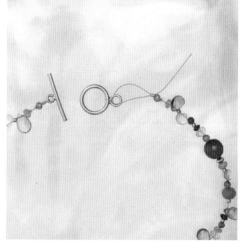

8 Secure the other end of the beaded wire to the second part of the clasp in the same way. Your stunning necklace is finished. Wear it with pride knowing that you created it yourself.

faceted crystal
beads make excellent
evening wear

gold-colour daisy
spacers provide
the glitz

you only need a
few bright beads
for impact

splash out on a
really lovely focal
bead – this is
smoky quartz

gold always
looks good

big and bold

The delicate beads in the Fiesta necklace
look wonderful but if you don't have any of
the beads already, you won't want to splash
out on the lot. Never fear: use the beads you
do have, even if they are much bigger, and
although the effect will be different, it will be
no less dramatic.

this large drop
makes an
excellent focus

pearls with a twist

Now that there are so many lovely pearls to choose from in every price range (see pages 38–39) it can be hard to decide just which ones you like best. This trendy twisted pearl necklace overcomes that problem by using three different types, and you can add more, if desired.

you will need

tools

Wire cutters
Crimping pliers

materials

Soft Flex beading wire or equivalent, or for real pearls use a thread and knot between each pearl (see pages 70–73)

40cm (16in) strand of mother-of-pearl chips

40cm (16in) strand of 4mm pearls (freshwater, real or fake)

40cm (16in) strand of 10mm pearls (real or fake)

Several handfuls of translucent seed beads

2 silver end cones about 18mm long and wide enough to take three strands of seed beads

Silver toggle clasp

Transparent sticky tape

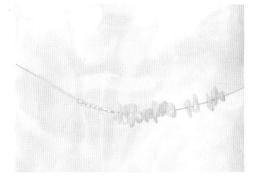

seed bead

1 Cut three pieces of beading wire at least 71cm (28in) long. Stick a piece of tape 5cm (2in) from one end of the first length to prevent the beads falling off and start by stringing on enough seed beads to match the length of the cone or a bit less – about 6–8 should be sufficient.

2 Now start stringing on your first bead type, such as mother-of-pearl chips. I used one type of pearl or shell for each strand, but you could mix and match your pearls, perhaps using several shades of the same type of bead for each strand.

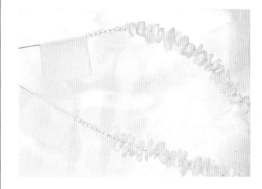

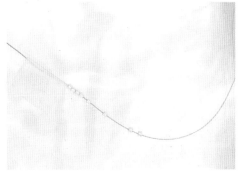

3 Finish stringing on the beads, adding the same number of seed beads at the end of the string as you did at the beginning. Now attach another piece of tape and set the strand to one side.

4 Pick up your second strand of beading wire, attach tape 5cm (2in) from one end and string on the seed beads as before. You may wish to use the same number as before or use a few more or less.

tip

Once you have strung up your first strand of beads, slip a cone onto the end and check that you like the effect. If you decide that there are too many seed beads protruding, take them off now and string up the remaining strands with a similarly reduced number of beads.

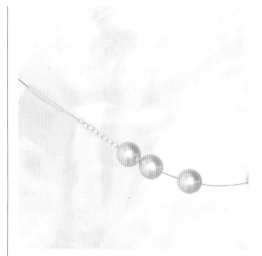

seed beads

5 Now string on your second main bead type, in this case the 10mm pearls. Thread on enough so that when you have added the seed pearls at the other end the strand will be the same length as your first strand.

6 Add the seed beads at the end and then apply a piece of tape to prevent the beads falling off.

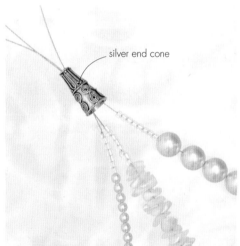

silver end cone

7 String up your third and final strand in exactly the same way as before, starting and finishing with seed beads. This time use your 4mm pearl beads.

8 Now for the tricky part. Take the tape off one end of each strand and pass all three wire ends through one of the cones, as shown. Hold tight – the last thing you want at this stage is to drop the beads.

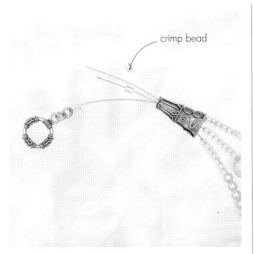

crimp bead

9 Use the crimping technique explained on pages 68–69 to connect each strand to the first part of the clasp, pulling the wire as tight as you can for a neat finish. This can be a little bit awkward, so take your time.

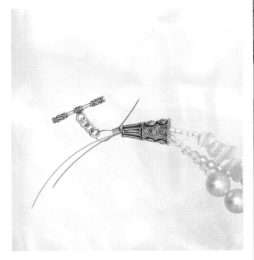

10 If desired, twist the strands of pearls together before adding the clasp to the other end. Experiment to see what looks best with your beads. Repeat steps 8–9 to attach the cone and second portion of the clasp to the other end of each strand.

fake it

Real pearls can look formal, so if they don't suit the occasion, try fakes. They come in some fabulous colours – both realistic and outrageous – and won't break the bank.

these beads have a glittery, almost powdery surface

make sure you have some small beads to fill in the gaps

these beads have an eye-catching metallic finish

a few large beads add to the textural effect

golden glow

There are few combinations as beautiful and luxurious as gold and amber, which is why this amber drop necklace is a real stunner. You only need eight amber beads but you will also require a length of really nice chunky chain, available from some jewellers by the metre (yard).

you will need

tools

Wire cutters

Needle-nose or chain-nose pliers

Round-nose or rosary pliers

materials

1 large oval amber bead about 20mm long

7 smaller amber beads about 10–15mm long, matched in pairs with one exception (see the photograph, left)

65cm (26in) of gold chain

1 long fine gold headpin and some fine gold-colour wire or 10 long gold headpins

16 gold-colour bead ends in a size to fit your beads

2 small gold beads

Gold clasp – I used an oval toggle clasp that complemented the oval chain links

curve facing upward

1 Each bead has a gold bead end on each side to create a luxurious look and cover the holes in the beads. Thread the first bead end onto a long, fine headpin with the curve facing upward, as shown.

2 Thread on your largest amber bead. It should sit nicely in the curve of the bead end. Thread on a second bead end with the curve facing toward the bead and push it down against the bead.

wrapped head pin

3 You can either attach this bead directly to the next one as shown in the main photograph (see left) or join it with a chain link (see step 4 photograph). To attach it directly to the next link, wire wrap it, (see pages 78–79). To use a link first clip a link from your chain, then wire wrap the bead to that link. Clip off the end of the headpin close to the wrapped wire.

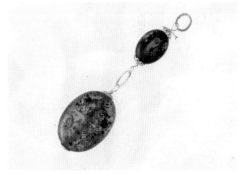

4 Take a 10cm (4in) length of wire or long headpin and slip on a bead end, the unpaired amber bead and a second bead end, with the bead ends curving towards the bead. Wire wrap it to the chain link attached to the first bead (or to the wrapped loop) then to a second single chain link following the instructions on pages 80–81.

three beads attached to one chain link

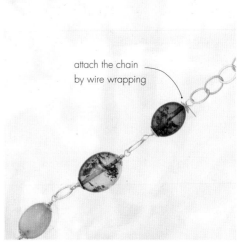

attach the chain by wire wrapping

5 Attach two identical beads to the link, each with a bead end on each side. Attach a link to the free end of each one, then another amber bead, another link and the final amber beads. You have created a beautiful Y-shaped piece with the large drop at the end.

6 Cut two 30cm (12in) lengths of chain, or your preferred length, and join one to each of the amber beads at the top of the necklace by wire wrapping as before. Trim the end of the wire close to the bead.

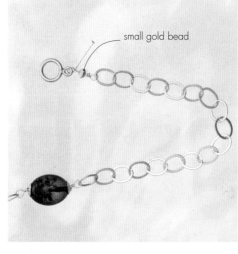

small gold bead

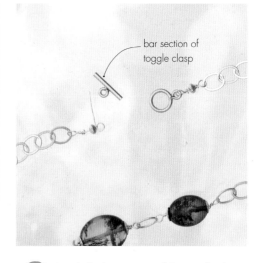

bar section of toggle clasp

7 Use a 5cm (2in) length of gold wire or a long headpin to wire wrap the free end of one chain to the ring section of the toggle clasp using a small gold bead as explained in detail on pages 80–81.

8 Attach the bar section of the toggle clasp to the other free end of chain in exactly the same way to complete a spectacular necklace that deserves pride of place in your jewellery box. You can feel proud of yourself.

warm and wonderful

You may not be able to obtain exactly the same materials as I used, or you might prefer other colours or materials. But whether you use amber or amethyst, semi-precious stones, glass beads or resin, this stunning design won't disappoint you.

tip

If you can't find one bead type in two or more sizes, as in my original necklace, you could simply use one size throughout, as I did with the glass-bead necklace below. Alternatively, choose a different type of bead entirely for the main drop, such as fabulous Murano glass, and use plainer coordinating beads for the others.

carnelians are far cheaper than amber beads but just as lovely

gold findings are wonderfully opulent

silver wire and bead ends were used here, but brass would tie in better with the beads.

these decorative glass beads have a ripple of metal running through for added brilliance

water world

Inspired by deep seas and tropical waters, this long necklace incorporates turquoise, wood, coral and quartz crystal interspersed with gold chain. It can be worn as one long single strand, double wrapped or even triple wrapped for a chunkier look. The hard work has a big pay-off at the end.

you will need

tools

Wire cutters

Crimping pliers

Needle-nose pliers

Rosary pliers

materials

Soft Flex beading wire or equivalent

About 14 turquoise nuggets approximately 20mm long

Sponge coral heshi wheel approximately 4–6mm long, or equivalent

14 irregular-shaped coral cylinder/barrel beads approximately 9mm long, or equivalent

8 brandy quartz crystal faceted rectangles about 10mm long

About 13 palmwood beads 6–8mm long and 6 palmwood beads 7–8mm long

4 large carved vermeil (gold) beads 10mm long

Vermeil (gold) daisy spacers

35cm (14in) of medium link gold-colour chain

Gold-colour crimp beads

Gold filigree oval clasp

24-gauge gold-colour wire and headpins

Transparent sticky tape

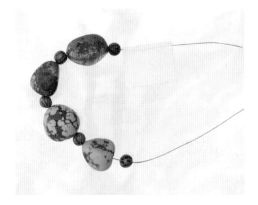

1 Cut seven pieces of 5cm (2in) chain. Although you don't need it all yet, it is easier to have it ready to go. Cut a short length of beading wire and string on some beads – I combined turquoise nuggets and palmwood.

connect here

2 Start attaching the beads to the first length of chain. To do this thread on a crimp bead then thread the wire through the first loop of the chain and back through the crimp bead. Pull tight and crimp (see pages 68–69).

wire wrap

3 On the other side of the chain wire wrap a bead to the end link, following the instructions on pages 78–81. If the bead is short, you can use a headpin for this but for longer beads you will need to use a length of gold-colour wire.

4 Keep adding beads in the same way until you have about 8–12cm (3–5in) of wrapped beads on the end of the chain. Add spacers or bead ends as desired for a luxurious effect.

tip

Not everyone is happy about the idea of using coral in their jewellery. There are plenty of alternatives that you could use instead, but if you want to stick with semi-precious stones, some lovely choices are carnelian, red jasper or even copper pearls. (Pearls come in some lovely hot colours and are surprisingly inexpensive if you buy the freshwater versions.)

5 Now you can attach another length of beading wire to the last wire-wrapped bead and thread on some more beads. Use a gold crimp bead to attach about 13–18cm (5–7in) of beading wire.

6 Thread on an arrangement of beads – I used a lovely combination of turquoise nuggets alternating with small coral heshi wheels. Your beaded string should be 8–13cm (3–5in) long.

7 Now it's time for another length of chain. Crimp the end of your beading wire to the first link in a piece of chain, pulling the beads tight before you do so. At the other end of the chain start adding wire-wrapped beads.

8 Sometimes you can wire wrap a group of beads, treating them as one, as shown here. In this case a gold headpin was used, but if your beads make up a longer length, you will need to use gold wire, which is also less expensive. If you are new to beading, cut a nice long length of the beading wire to give you plenty to play with.

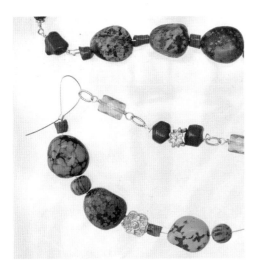

tip

If your wire wrapping looks unskilled, it could be because your wire is too thick. The finer your gold wire or headpins, the neater your wire wrapping will be. However, if you go too fine your jewellery will become extremely delicate. I found 24-gauge wire to be ideal.

9 After you have added about 8–13cm (3–5in) of wrapped beads you can add more strung beads, crimping them to the last wrapped bead, as shown. This time I added a range of beads, including a vermeil bead that will balance the gold clasp.

10 Continue in the same way, adding gold chain, wire-wrapped beads and threaded beads and placing the large vermeil beads every 20–40cm (8–16in). Space any other distinctive beads evenly around the necklace too.

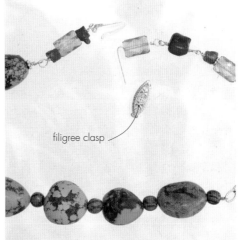

filigree clasp

11 This finished necklace is 127cm (50in) long, so continue adding beads until you reach this length or as desired, finishing with wire-wrapped beads at each end to ensure that you can attach the clasp neatly and easily.

12 Attach one part of the clasp to each end of the necklace by wire wrapping. I chose a filigree clasp so it would be camouflaged in the necklace and could be worn in front, if desired. This was a difficult project and you're done. Now go wear it super-long to your waist or wrap it around and around for a completely different look.

island dream

Shady palm trees, golden beaches, soothing ocean breezes and sunshine will all be conjured up while making this shell necklace, which features a lovely shell pendant, shimmering mother-of-pearl beads and citrine nuggets to capture the warmth of the sun.

you will need

tools

Wire cutters
Crimping pliers

materials

112cm (44in) length of Soft Flex beading wire or equivalent

Shell pendant about 48mm long

4 citrine nuggets about 12–16mm long

Large handful of 4mm yellow seed beads to link back to the colour of the citrines

Large handful of 4mm round mother-of-pearl beads

2 gold-colour crimp beads

Gold-colour lobster clasp

50mm length of medium-link gold chain

Short length of gold-colour wire

Transparent sticky tape

1 My necklace has two 46cm (18in) strands so I cut two 56cm (22in) lengths of beading wire to allow for crimping the ends. Thread each strand through the shell pendant and slide it to the centre.

2 Bring the two ends of one length of wire together with the ends matching and string on the nuggets. If desired, add seed beads between them as I did for the version shown in the photograph left.

mother-of-pearl

3 At this point separate the strands and string each one individually. Bead one string first, working to a regular pattern or randomly. I combined yellow seed beads and mother-of-pearl beads. When the string is 22.5cm (9in) long stick a piece of tape over the end.

4 String up the second strand in the same way, using the same type of pattern – either random or regular – as for the first strand. When the beaded strand is the same length as the first strand stick a piece of tape over the end to prevent the beads falling off.

The pendant is the dominant feature of this necklace. Buy this first and choose the other beads to match. I used citrine beads to evoke the warmth of sun and sand, but if this colour does not go well with your pendant then do not hesitate to choose a different stone.

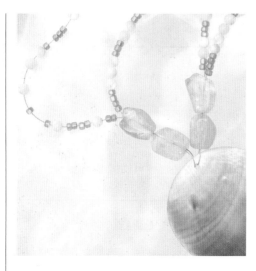

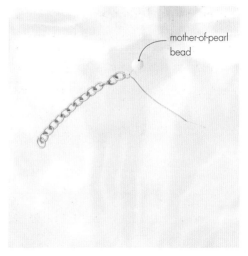

mother-of-pearl bead

5 Referring to steps 2–4, thread up the second length of beading wire in exactly the same way, starting with a balanced pair of citrine nuggets, as shown.

6 Slip a bead onto a gold-colour headpin and wire wrap it to the 50mm (2in) length of gold chain, as shown, following the instructions on pages 78–79. I used a mother-of-pearl bead, but use whatever bead you like best.

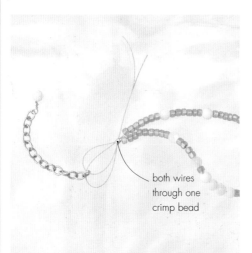

both wires through one crimp bead

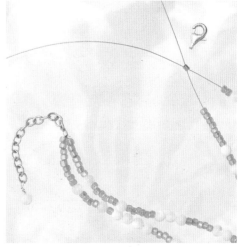

7 Attach the other end of the chain to the two ends of one of your beading wires. To do this, slip both ends through a crimp bead then through the end link on the chain and back through the crimp bead. Pull up tight and use your crimping pliers to flatten the crimp bead (see pages 68–69 for further details).

8 Pass the two remaining lengths of wire through a second crimp bead, as shown. Pass them through the loop in the lobster clasp and back through the crimp bead. Crimp as before to complete your dream necklace.

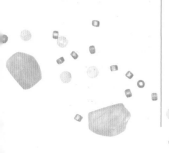

little and large

This necklace design works with all sorts of pendants or medallions, whether made of shell or something completely different, and in almost any size and shape. The rectangular pendant on the right has an elegant look when paired with beads in two colours, while the large medallion below left has a funky style that goes so well with its metallic thong.

small crystal beads in two colours pick up the pattern of the pendant

a silver thong adds sparkle in an instant

these bone-style beads work very well here

this large modern pendant bead has a minimalist treatment

tip

Make your own pendant for this design by threading a large bead on a long headpin and wire-wrapping the end following the instructions on pages 78–79. Then thread your two beading wires through the loop you made in the wire and off you go.

quick & easy
designs

all about the projects

Many of Maya Brenner's designs, featured on the previous pages, are quite quick to make, but if you want something really easy to get you started then choose from this collection by Gunilla Johansson. It's inspired by Maya's jewellery and ideal for the beginner. Each project is completed in just four simple steps.

This collection of earrings, bracelets and necklaces has been tried and tested by beginners, so if you are lacking in confidence, then this is the place to start.

incredibly easy earrings

All four of the earring designs in this section are easy, and absolutely anyone can make the bead hoops (pages 158–159) and leaf hoops (pages 160–161) which are so simple you don't even need any specialized tools. All of these projects can be completed in less than 30 minutes, and some in much less time.

brilliantly basic bracelets

The bracelets will take a little longer than the earrings to make simply because more beads are involved. However, you won't need any tools for the memory wire bracelet on pages 166–167 and because of their chunky beads, the seed pod and wooden bracelets on pages 168–171 can be completed in no time.

nothing-to-them necklaces

The necklaces are the most complicated pieces in this section because you need to add the clasps and you'll be using a lot of beads, but when you break the projects down into stages you'll find that they are really straightforward. Even the exotic multi-strand necklace on

pages 176–177 is easy when you know how. All you have to do is string up four strands of different lengths with whatever beads you like and then attach them to the clasp. It really couldn't be simpler.

natural beauty
Featuring seeds, metal, glass and leather, this example of nature's wonders is surprisingly quick to make. The chain makes it easily adjustable too.

earring projects

gypsy maiden

158–159

garden fairy

160–161

tiger woman

162–163

pearly queen

164–165

bracelet projects

indian princess

166–167

fire goddess

168–169

wood nymph

170–171

desert diva

172–173

necklace projects

aztec explorer

174–175

eastern empress

176–177

blue bird

178–179

african queen

180–181

gypsy maiden

These chunky hoop earrings can't help but draw attention to themselves. They are relaxed and easy to wear and you can make them in less than half an hour. The beads aren't fixed in place so you can easily change them to suit every mood or occasion.

you will need

tools

Needle-nose or chain-nose pliers (optional)

materials

Large gold-colour ear hoops – these are 40mm (1¾in) wide

2 brown seed pods

4 x 14mm discs in cork, bone or wood

4 x 6mm glass beads in warm yellow

4 x 4mm beads in cork, bone or wood

8 seed beads

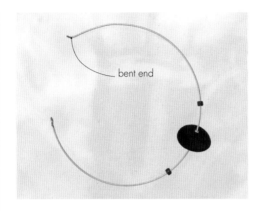

1. Take one of the hoops and slip on a seed bead, a disc and then another seed bead. If you find it difficult to get the beads on the hoop, you may need to straighten out the bend in the end slightly with your pliers.

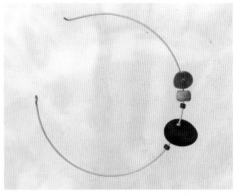

2. Slide on one of the 4mm beads followed by a 6mm yellow bead, which takes you to the centre. For a fuller look add additional beads of your choice.

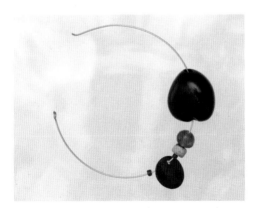

3. Add the focal bead, in this case a brown seed pod. These have the advantage of being large but light, so you get impact without having to weigh down your ears.

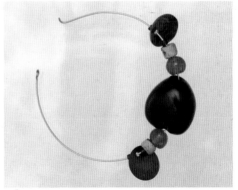

4. Now repeat the bead pattern in reverse order, adding a 6mm yellow bead, 4mm bead, seed bead, disc and then the final seed bead. Repeat on the second earring. If necessary, bend the wire end back into position.

garden fairy

This is a pretty pastoral variation of the gypsy hoops featured on pages 158–159. In this case the hoop fits into a connector which is then attached to an ear wire. The beads are permanently sealed inside the hoop so they are less likely to go astray.

you will need

tools

Needle-nose or chain-nose pliers

materials

2 x 40mm (1¾in) silver-colour hoops

2 silver ear wires

2 x 25mm green leaf pendants

4 x 12mm green leaf drops

4 blue 8mm round glass pendants

4 red 8mm glass pendants

4 x 6mm green faceted beads – these were made of hurricane glass

4 x 3mm silver beads

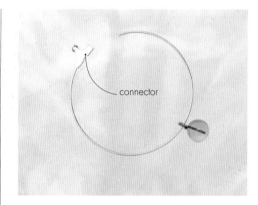

1 Pull the wire hoop beside the small triangular connector. One of the ends will slip out so that you can slide on the beads. Start by slipping on one of the 8mm round blue pendant beads.

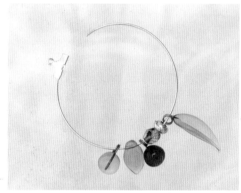

2 Add a small leaf followed by a red bead and then a 6mm faceted bead. Then slide on the first silver bead, followed by the 12mm leaf pendant.

3 Work back in reverse order, adding a silver bead, faceted bead, the red drop, small leaf and then the blue drop to complete the beading, as shown.

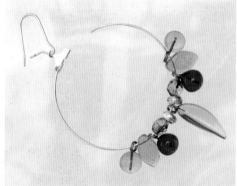

4 Slip the ear wire through the loop on the connector. Now push the end of the hoop back into place, deep into the connector. Use your pliers to squeeze the connector around the wire end to secure it. Repeat to make the second earring in the same way.

tiger woman

Tiger's eye was worn by Roman soldiers into battle because they believed it offered protection. It is also thought to focus the mind and relieve high blood pressure, but even without these assets it's a lovely stone worthy of your attention. Here gold findings enhance its natural warmth.

you will need

tools

Crimping pliers

materials

20cm (8in) of Soft Flex beading wire or equivalent

2 x 12mm oval tiger's eye beads

4 x 6mm round tiger's eye beads

2 large gold-colour daisy spacers

2 small gold-colour daisy spacers

6 gold beads

4 gold crimp beads

2 gold ear wires – these were fishhooks

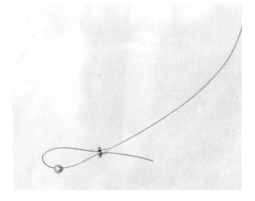

1 Cut the beading wire in half. Thread one piece through a crimp bead, then a small daisy spacer and a gold bead. Thread back through the spacer and crimp bead. Pull tight and crimp the bead (see pages 68–69).

2 Trim off the short end of wire or conceal the end inside the next bead. Thread on a 6mm round tiger's eye bead followed by the large gold-colour daisy spacer and then the 12mm oval tiger's eye bead.

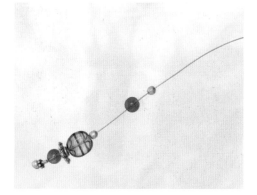

3 Add a round gold bead followed by a second 6mm round tiger's eye bead and then another gold bead. Hold the wire up to your ear and check that you are happy with the effect. If not, make your changes now.

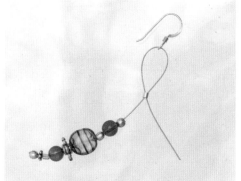

4 Slip on a crimp bead, slide the beaded wire through the ring in an ear wire and then take it back through the crimp bead. Pull up tight and crimp the bead in the usual way (see pages 68–69). Make the second earring in the same way to finish.

pearly queen

Abalone is surely the queen of shells, shimmering with every colour from pink to blue, green and grey as it catches the light. These simple earrings make a feature of the large square abalone beads, which are combined here with mother-of-pearl chips to continue the shell theme.

you will need

tools

Crimping pliers

materials

20cm (8in) of Soft Flex beading wire or equivalent

2 x 18mm flat square beads – these are abalone

4 small round silver beads

2 clear seed beads

2 mother-of-pearl chips

4 silver crimp beads

2 silver ear wires – these were ballposts with earnuts (butterfly clips)

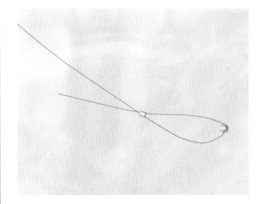

1 Cut the beading wire in half. Thread one piece through a silver-colour crimp bead and then a small silver bead. Take the wire back through the crimp bead, as shown. Pull tight and crimp the bead (see pages 68–69).

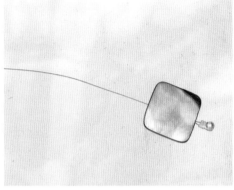

2 Trim off the short end of wire. If you wish you can leave a short length for strength and conceal it inside the large square bead, which you should thread on next.

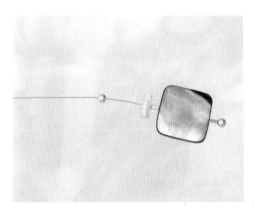

3 Thread on a small clear seed bead followed by one of the mother-of-pearl chips. Now add a round silver bead.

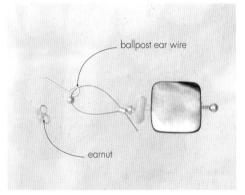

ballpost ear wire

earnut

4 Now thread on a silver crimp bead. Slip the wire through the loop on your ear wire and then back through the crimp bead, as shown. Pull up tight and crimp the bead in the usual way (see pages 68–69). Make the second earring in the same way to finish.

indian princess

Memory wire is thick wire, coiled like a spring, which snaps back into its original form when pulled up and then released – in other words, it remembers its formed shape. Here it is used to make an effervescent bracelet that looks like several bangles worn together, Indian style.

you will need

tools

Beading glue
Wire cutter

materials

Bracelet-length silver-colour memory wire

Turquoise seed beads

Handful of turquoise rondells 3–4mm across

9 faceted crystal or glass beads 8–10mm across in a ruby colour

8 faceted silver beads 5–6mm across

18 silver spacers

Transparent sticky tape

1 Take the ball off one end of the wire and slide on your beads; if the balls are already off, use tape to prevent the beads sliding off. Slip on the seed beads, faceted beads and daisy spacers first.

2 Keep adding the beads. This bracelet features different beads in the centre of the bracelet for variety and colour. Try adding some turquoise rondells, as shown here.

3 Continue to build up the design. Having added the rondells, return to the same pattern of beads used at the start, combining the seed beads with the faceted beads and silver daisy spacers.

4 Complete the design. When you can no longer fit any more beads on the wire, add the ball ends. These should be glued in place with a little beading glue.

fire goddess

Seed pods make excellent beads. They are lightweight, colourful and large enough to build up a design quickly (and inexpensively). Their chunky, up-to-the-minute look works especially well when strung on thongs, as shown here. Funky bracelets like this one are also great fun to make.

you will need

tools

Scissors

materials

Suede thong in a natural shade of brown or your preferred stringing material, such as raffia or rat's tail

6 red seed pods

9 wooden beads 1cm long with holes large enough for the thong to go through

1 Cut a length of suede thong about twice the desired measurement of the finished bangle. Tie an overhand knot in the centre of the thong and slide on a wooden bead. Tie a second knot on the other side of the bead.

2 Working outward on both sides, slide on a seed pod and then knot the thong again, so that each seed pod is held in place by a knot on each side.

3 Continue the pattern until the bracelet is the desired length. Add another wooden bead to each end (see step 4) if you want to create a little extra length.

4 When you are happy with the size of the bracelet, securely knot the two ends and trim the thong close to the knot, but not right up against it or it will come undone. Vary this pattern by using orange seed pods and 20mm glass cone beads (see right), if you wish.

wood nymph

Some people think that they should only use one bead type in a project for it to work successfully, or that they have to use beads of a similar size or structure. This project shows that thinking outside the box, and using a mix-and-match approach can work well, too.

you will need

tools

Wire cutters
Crimping pliers

materials

30cm (12in) of Soft Flex beading wire or equivalent

3 flat wood and shell pendants 30mm across

4 round wooden beads 20mm across

2 gold hexagonal beads 20mm across

10 faceted crystal beads 8mm across, clear or fire-polished

10 large gold-colour spacer beads

2 gold-colour crimp beads

Gold-colour toggle clasp

1 Start stringing this bracelet at the centre and work outward to each side. This way you will be better able to judge the effect of the pattern as you go along. Thread one of the pendant beads onto the beading wire.

2 On each side of this add a crystal bead then a spacer, a wooden bead and a second spacer. Now add another crystal bead and then a gold hexagon, as shown.

3 Continue adding beads to each side until you reach the desired length. Then add another crystal bead, a spacer, a crystal, a pendant, a crystal, a spacer, another wooden bead and then a final spacer.

4 Now all that remains is to attach the clasp. At each end thread on a crimp bead then pass the wire through one section of the clasp and back through the crimp bead. Pull up tight and crimp the bead following the instructions on pages 68–69.

desert diva

There's nothing like a multi-strand for opulence and outrageousness, but what is one doing in the Quick & Easy section? The answer is that it really isn't hard to make and you don't need to spend hours threading it. Choose a single colour and your design is bound to look great.

you will need

tools

Wire cutters

Crimping pliers

materials

90cm (3ft) of Soft Flex beading wire or equivalent

1 large briolette about 20mm long

2 rectangular beads 15mm long

2 flat round beads 10mm long

4 briolettes 8–10mm long

2 round beads 8mm across

Approximately 13 yellow faceted crystal beads 8mm across

2 square flat beads 8mm across

Yellow-gold seed beads

Gold-colour clasp

6 gold-colour crimp beads

Transparent sticky tape

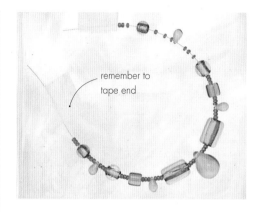

remember to tape end

1 Cut three 30cm (12in) lengths of beading wire. Stick tape over one end of the first length and string on the beads in any order you like. This bracelet features a symmetrical design about 18cm (7¼in) long. Tape the end.

2 Take your second length of beading wire and stick tape over one end. String up this length using a different bead arrangement. Tape the end, as before, when it is the same length as the first.

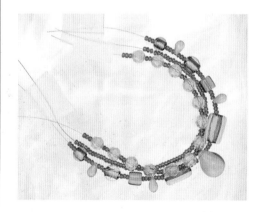

3 String up your final strand. Since this piece was looking sufficiently chunky already, the final strand does not need a lot of large beads. Instead, the third strand consists of seed beads only.

4 Now add the clasp by crimping each strand to each section of the clasp following the instructions on pages 68–69. Make sure you attach one strand at a time and that the strands aren't twisted unless that's the way you want them to be.

aztec explorer

Whether you yearn to explore the jungles of Mexico or know you'll never get farther than the park, this casual necklace will fuel your dreams. The chunky beads and simple stringing technique mean that you can complete this necklace in well under an hour.

you will need

tools

Tweezers

Needle-nose or chain-nose pliers

Round-nose pliers or rosary pliers

Wire cutters

Scissors or snips

materials

Length of brown leather thong

10 dark brown seed pod beads

5 blue glass nugget-style beads 20mm long

5 decorative gold or brass beads 20mm long

Small bead to decorate the end of the extension chain

8cm (3in) length of gold-colour chain

Gold-colour headpin

2 gold-colour jumprings

Gold-colour lobster clasp

1 Tie an overhand knot in the thong about 5cm (2in) from one end. Thread on a seed pod bead and tie another knot close to the bead (see pages 70–73). Use tweezers to help position the knot close to the bead.

2 Thread on a gold bead and tie another knot. Add a seed pod, tie a knot and then add a blue glass bead. This is your pattern – repeat the sequence in steps 1 and 2 until you have used all your beads.

jumpring

3 Open a jumpring and slip it through the small hole in the lobster clasp. Close the ring and knot one end of the necklace to it tightly, adjacent to the first knot. Trim the thong close to the first knot and trim the other end, leaving a long enough piece to tie a double knot.

jumpring

4 Wire wrap the small bead to one end of the chain (see pages 78–79). Attach the second jumpring to the other end of the chain and close the ring. Slip the free end of the necklace through the jumpring and knot securely, as before. Trim off the excess thong.

eastern empress

OK, so this necklace isn't all that quick to make, but it's certainly easy – the sort of thing you can run up while half your mind is engrossed in a TV show. Set out piles of beads in a selected range of colours and before you know it you'll have produced a masterpiece.

you will need

tools

Wire cutters

Crimping pliers

materials

Soft Flex beading wire or equivalent

Lots of beads in a narrow range of colours: reds, yellows and oranges; pinks, reds and purples; or blues, greens and turquoise

Lobster clasp

Jumpring or clasp fitting

2 large crimp beads (see step 4)

Transparent sticky tape

1 Cut five lengths of beading wire. The finished strands here will be 46cm (18in), 48cm (18¾in), 50cm (19½in), 52cm (20¼in) and 54cm (21in), but cut each strand 10cm (4in) longer to allow for adding the clasp.

remember to tape end

2 Stick a piece of tape 5cm (2in) from the end of the shortest length and start stringing on the beads in a pleasing yet random pattern. When the strand is the desired length stick another piece of tape over the end.

3 String up the remaining four strands of beading wire in the same way. It sometimes helps to lay out the completed strand(s) in front of you as you work, so you can ensure that they look good together.

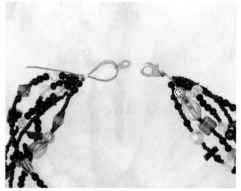

4 Five crimp beads would be very bulky beside the small clasp used here, so all five strands are strung through the one large crimp bead, then through the clasp and back through the bead. Crimp in the usual way (see pages 68–69).

blue bird

This necklace was inspired by the lariat on page 126 but the small loop on the end means that you require far fewer beads because you don't need to double it up. The simple beading design is really quick to follow and ideal for the beginner because no specialized tools are required.

you will need

tools

Scissors or snips
Beading glue

materials

Transparent or silver-colour beading thread

1 x 30mm clear/white oval nugget bead

1 x 20mm flat blue glass oval bead

1 x 12mm clear/white bead

2 x 15mm oval blue glass beads

4 x 14–15mm clear/white nuggets

3 x 12mm decorative blue glass beads

3 x 10mm brown oval glass beads

4 x 7mm clear/white round beads

4 x 7mm brown round beads

3 x 7mm blue round beads

1 x 7mm yellow round bead

Handful of brown seed beads

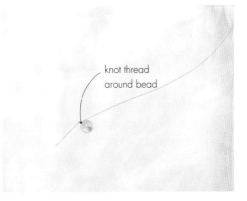

knot thread around bead

1 Cut a 90cm (1yd) length of clear nylon beading thread or silver wire. This will give you plenty to play with. Tie on the first bead, a 7mm clear round bead, near one end with a double knot, as shown.

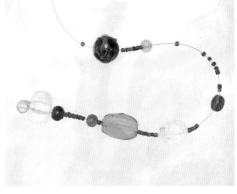

2 Now get stringing, starting with a clear 20mm bead and separating the large beads with random numbers of seed beads. Use the pictures as reference if you wish to copy this design, or create your own pattern.

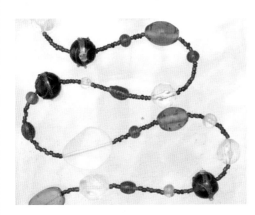

3 Space out the largest, most decorative beads fairly evenly while maintaining the relaxed look. Continue stringing on the beads until the lariat is the required length – about 66cm (26in) or whatever length suits you.

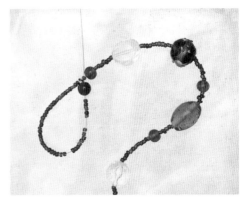

4 String on about 8cm (3in) of seed beads and then a 7mm brown bead. Pass the thread through one or two of the first seed beads on this section, pull it up tightly and make a double knot. Trim off the end and secure with a little glue to finish.

african queen

With its beautiful African turquoise beads it's easy to see where this necklace got its name. To enhance the African theme some chunky metal beads are also used, some with a jewelled surface to echo the colours of the turquoise. The cone ends are purely decorative.

you will need

tools

Wire cutters
Crimping pliers

materials

Soft Flex beading wire or equivalent

40cm (16in) string of 8mm round African turquoise beads

40cm (16in) string of 6mm round African turquoise beads

4 x 18–20mm silver bicones

3 jewelled round metal beads about 15mm across

2 silver-colour cone ends (optional)

Silver S-clasp

Transparent sticky tape

1 Cut a 90cm (1yd) length of beading wire for stringing. Stick tape over one end and begin threading on the 6mm and 8mm turquoise beads alternately.

2 Thread on 21 beads, as shown, with each 6mm bead followed by an 8mm bead except the last one. Now add an 18mm silver bead and continue stringing, starting with a 6mm bead, as before.

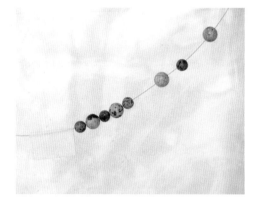

3 When you have added nine of the turquoise beads string on a jewelled metal bead and then add nine more turquoise beads. As before, start and end with a smaller, 6mm bead, as shown.

4 Add a large silver bead then continue stringing, placing the decorative beads nine turquoise beads apart and using the photograph opposite as a guide. Finish with 21 turquoise beads. At each end slip on the cone end then attach the clasp (see pages 68–69).

inspiring colour themes

all about colour

Do you put together interesting and exciting colour combinations with so much ease that it is almost an unconscious process? Are you able to mix colours that other people wouldn't dream of combining and still create something spectacular and enviable? If not, read on for some easy ways to colour success.

Many of us have favourite colours that we return to again and again throughout our lives – our comfort colours. At other times we choose according to mood or season. But there are times when we want something more exciting than the norm, more stimulating and vibrant. If you know you want something more but don't know where to start, consider turning to one of the following combinations.

creative combinations

One-colour theme Choose beads in a single colour, adding variety through shape and tone (see Eye of the Tiger, pages 106–107 and Purple Reigns, pages 122–125).

Colour families Limit yourself to two or three colours adjacent to each other on the colour wheel for a gentle harmony. Blue, turquoise and green, for example, yellow, orange and red, or blue through purple to red (see Island Dream on pages 150–153 and the multi-strand necklace on pages 176–177).

Complementary colours These are colours opposite each other on the colour wheel that, when placed together, make each other appear brighter and bolder. Try combining yellow with purple, green with red, and blue with orange for the brightest contrasts. For a subtler effect choose less of a contrast as in the ever popular combination of blue and yellow.

Themes These are a great way of devising a colour story. Simply think of a theme, such as rainforest, angel or fire and then select colours, patterns and textures that you feel fulfil the brief. Pages 186–205 provide some samples to get you started. Don't worry about authenticity too much here. Your idea of what constitutes a particular theme may well be different to the next person's. That doesn't matter. The point is that the theme gets you thinking about colours that work well together, and as a bonus they often lead you to consider other aspects, such as whether the beads are shiny or matte, plain or textured.

colour store
Store beads by colour (right) so you can easily find coordinating combinations.

rainbow
This necklace contains all the colours of the rainbow. Notice how the colours drift from one to the next in a restful way yet the overall effect is both lively and energizing.

fire

For passion and energy combine reds, oranges,
yellows and gold. Use gold-colour beading wire,
chain and findings to complement their warm tones.

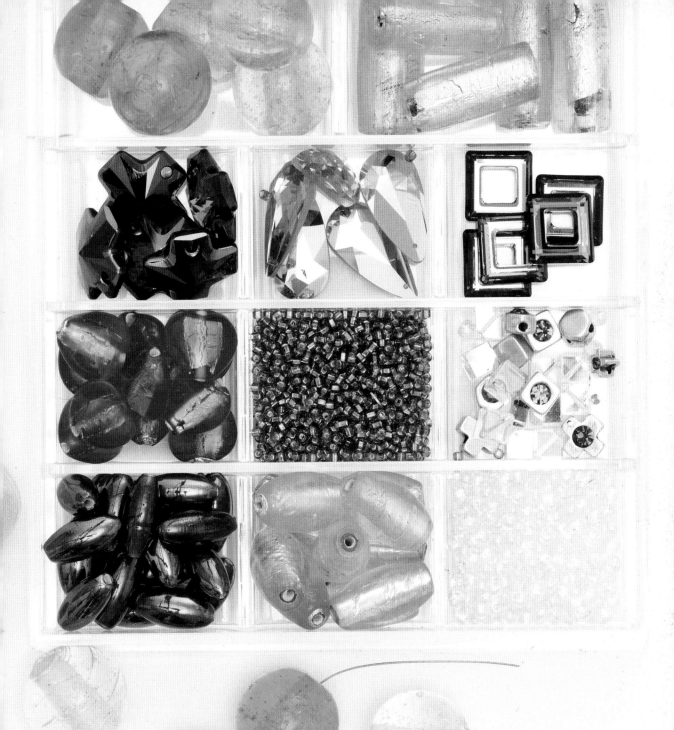

ice

Channel your inner Grace Kelly using the cool tones shown in this colour chart for inspiration. Choose from a palette of regal blues, frosty lilacs, and shimmering crystals to create jewellery with an icy look.

angel

Throughout history white and shades of
cream have been linked with virtue in the
Western world. Add golds, pearls or
shimmering fire-polished crystals to get more
than a few feathers flying.

vixen

"When I'm good, I'm very good, but when I'm bad I'm better."

If, like Mae West, you're in a mood to be wicked, what better

than the combination of black, red and metallic colours?

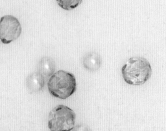

princess

You'll look as pretty as a princess when you mix frosty colours with soft

pinks, purples and peaches. Add some clear beads for that girlish sparkle

or some mirrored or fire-polished beads.

boho

Reveal your colourful character by wearing wild
and wacky beads or mixing bright, contrasting
colours like this blinding combination of red
and blue. Pull them all together in a multi-strand
for greatest impact.

peacock

With their fabulous jewelled plumage, peacocks strut among their fellows like kings. Take inspiration from them and queen it over your peers in your own confection made in peacock blues, greens and purples.

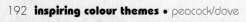

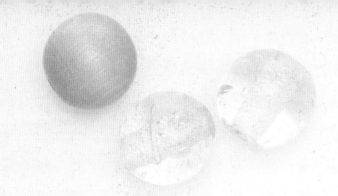

dove

Gentle as the dove, shades of beige, cream and white combine to produce jewellery of subtle beauty that will go with almost anything and can be worn anywhere with confidence.

party girl

Sparkle, glitter and glitz are what you need to shine at a party, so look out for all those lovely mirrored beads and the foiled or frosted glass and combine them with plenty of gold and silver for a glamorous look.

earth mother

Look at this mouth-watering selection of beads made from natural materials including wood, bone, stone and ceramic (clay), and you'll wonder why man ever bothered with synthetics. What better way to get back in touch with the cosmos than with a piece of jewellery that celebrates nature's little luxuries?

vintage

This theme is all about capturing the glamour of bygone eras, their opulence and richness, so go for gold and sumptuous beads. Size and colour really aren't important as long as the overall effect is luxurious and lavish.

modern

If this is your look then you are into minimalist chic. Colours to choose are neutrals like white, cream, black and grey, and the beads should be simple yet exquisite. You'll design a piece that's a modern classic.

'50s chic

History is a good place to find inspiration for your jewellery. This little collection was inspired by the ice-lolly colours favoured by young ladies in the 1950s – think of all those figure-hugging sweaters in *Grease*.

swinging '60s

The 1960s was when Mary Quant introduced the idea of affordable fashion to the exploding youth market. Suddenly it was not just OK to be young, it was essential. Colours were about making statements and being heard. So make a statement with your jewellery, using some of those snazzy beads you never could resist.

waterfall

Blues are universally popular, but simply stringing up a load of blue beads won't ensure that you create an object of beauty. Splash out on some gorgeous blue glass beads to combine with clear crystals and other sparkly bits, and dive into the creative process.

rainforest

Capture jungle abundance by combining blues and greens of every
description, adding textures and pearlized beads to represent reptiles,
and flashes of colour for the birds.

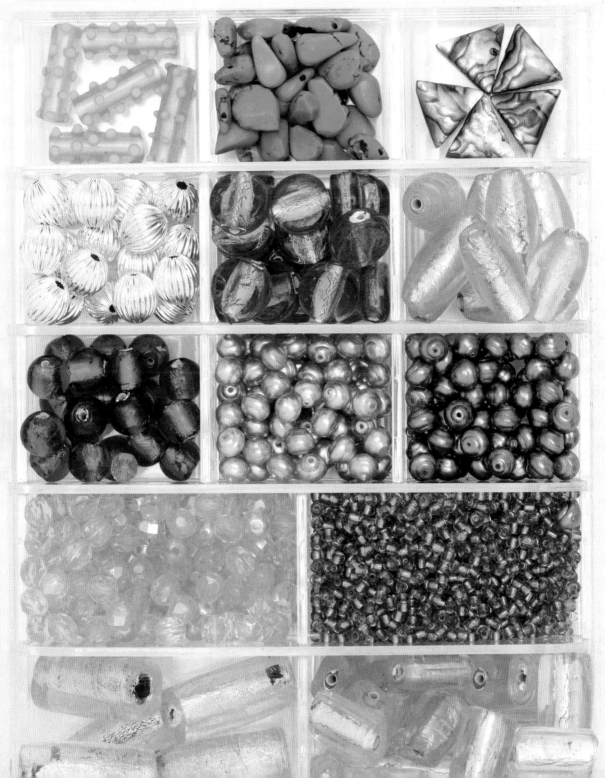

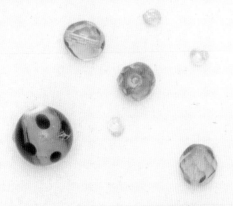

bollywood

Invoke Indian exoticism with the spicy colours of saffron, paprika and turmeric, and stir in some gold for dazzle. String up the beads by the dozen, with multi-strands galore for a truly sumptuous Bollywood effect.

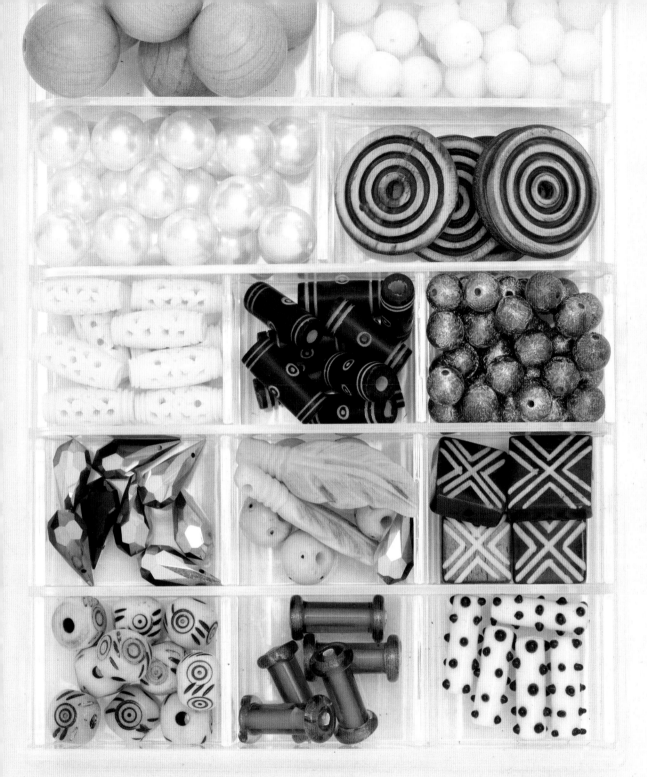

hollywood

Marilyn Monroe, Rita Hayworth, Ingrid Bergman, Bette Davis and other

leading ladies of the 1940s and '50s combined strength of personality

with femininity. Do the same with sexy, smoky colours and soft creams.

storm

Capture the power of wind and rain, thunder and lightning with metallics, greys, greens and steely blues, and show that you, too, are a force to be reckoned with.

rainbow

After the storm comes the sun, and with it a
rainbow. Inspiring and uplifting, a rainbow is
a symbol of hope, joy, forgiveness, spirituality
and happy endings. For the full effect keep the
colours in order: violet, indigo, blue, green,
yellow, orange and red, but add additional
shades in between, as desired.

trouble-
shooting

cleaning

If you're like me, you never take your jewellery off, which means you're guilty of wearing it in the shower, while cleaning the house, when gardening or preparing dinner. After a while this will cause the jewellery to lose some of its lustre and shine and it's time to take action.

Not all jewellery is alike and therefore maintenance differs for each. Here is a run-down of the basics.

silver

Silver should be rinsed in warm water and patted dry. If it is tarnished, use a silver-polishing cloth or a silver-cleaning fluid. For jewellery with intricate designs, use a silver-cleaning paste, which can get into small crevices. Don't use a toothbrush or other abrasives because they will scratch the surface. Wipe with a clean, soft cloth.

When travelling or in a rush, you can use toothpaste to clean silver and that works too!

gold

Soak gold for about 15 minutes in 240ml (two cups) of warm water with a few drops of mild washing-up liquid. Gently scrub with a soft-bristle toothbrush. Rinse with warm water and dry with a soft cloth.

gemstones

The safest way to clean gems is with plain warm water. If you feel that soap is necessary, use a mild liquid soap. Then rinse them and lay them on a soft towel to dry. Be aware that if your gems are on thread, the water may cause stretching or breakage. Some stones need special care. Amber, for example, should never go near ammonia or any hot solutions. Turquoise, lapis, malachite and onyx should only be cleaned with a soft damp cloth, since some detergents can discolour them. Many beads are dyed; rub your finger over the bead to see if any colour comes off. If it does, it should not be put in water.

pearls

Rub pearls individually with a soft, clean cloth dampened with a solution of 240ml (two cups) warm water and a few drops of a mild detergent. Don't soak them because this can cause the string to stretch. Air-dry overnight.

wash with care
When washing most jewellery only use plain water or add a little mild liquid soap.

precious piece

Most jewellery is a mix of materials. Wash briefly in plain lukewarm water, adding a tiny amount of gentle liquid soap if necessary. Pat dry with a clean, soft cloth or leave to dry naturally.

mending

Chances are that your jewellery will need repair at some point. Threads fray, weaken and then break, wires tend to bend and become brittle and springs inside clasps wear out – it's normal. But now, with your new beading skills, you can repair almost anything.

Clasps are the items that tend to go before any other part of the jewellery as they are used the most. Taking a necklace or bracelet on and off repeatedly will put strain on the area surrounding the clasp. The same goes for earrings and ear wires. However, if you've learned the skills in this book, then you have what it takes to fix almost anything and replacing the clasp will be child's play even if it wasn't you who made the piece of jewellery in the first place.

Threaded necklaces and bracelets, whether on silk, nylon or beading wire, can be restrung. Depending on where it breaks and how long the item is, you may have enough wire or string to re-crimp or re-knot the end without having to make the whole piece again. This may require that you make the piece a little shorter so that you have sufficient stringing material to enable you to complete the crimping process.

Chain items, such as the chandelier earrings on pages 96–97 or the drop necklace on pages 142–145 can be repaired simply by redoing the wire wrap that attaches the beads or clasp to the chain. It's that simple.

Earrings that break usually require a replacement ear wire or wire wrapping a bead with a new headpin. I've actually had more customers lose one earring and need to replace it than have a breakage, so you might consider saving extra beads when you make your earrings in case of loss, or even making a spare!

highly strung
When using thread or thongs it's a good idea to knot between each bead not only as a design feature but also to secure as many beads as possible should a breakage occur. You may still need to restring the whole piece but at least you'll have all the beads to do it with.

no knots

These pearls would have stayed put if the maker had knotted between each bead, a sensible precaution when the beads are valuable pearls or semi-precious stones. What's more, the knots help to protect the pearls and stop them rubbing together and damaging each other.

restoring & recycling

People have been recycling jewellery for years. The tradition is to take family heirlooms, such as your grandmother's engagement ring, and get them re-set. While you might not want to cut up priceless family heirlooms, you can take your old jewellery and make it new again.

If you've been making jewellery for any amount of time you've probably amassed quite a collection. Over time, your skills develop and styles change and you eventually end up with lots of jewellery that you no longer like.

Earrings are easily updated by changing ear wires from plain to fancy or making hoops out of drops. Even a simple thing like exchanging old findings for new gold or silver ones can make a marked improvement.

Bracelets that you no longer wear, perhaps in a single strand, can be combined to make flamboyant multi-strand confections with a totally updated look. Try adding charms or dangles for extra pizzazz.

Necklaces can be easily updated by adding an exciting new pendant to a plain necklace. I've done this plenty of times and it makes tired old necklaces look like new. You can turn a strung necklace into a wire-wrapped

extravaganza or even switch from silver findings to gold. I've also completely scrapped necklaces for their beads and components and just used them up in different designs. Whatever you decide to do, you are restoring the beads to their original beauty and hopefully getting more wear out of them – until you decide to change again.

recycling
This necklace was no longer appreciated, but some of the beads went to good use in a modern chunky bracelet, far right.

look around
Buttons from an old cardigan give an unusual twist to this pretty bracelet.

storage solutions

Beading is a messy business. The beads roll, bounce, drop, and hide in every nook and cranny. Not to mention all the pieces of wire that somehow end up on the floor and under my husband's bare feet. Storing your beads in an organized manner will not only save you time, it can help with your creativity.

Some people like to store their beads by colour, or by size, or by shape. Whatever method you choose, make sure you have easy access to your supplies, otherwise it can be very frustrating. Being able to see all your beads and stones together, and having easy access to them, can help you make important decisions about colour choices, sizes, textures, designs and so on.

storage options

Boxes are an obvious storage solution. A good bead storage container is clear and allows for stacking. For seed beads use a bead container that enables you to remove the cap and pour out beads from one section of the container while the other beads stay safely in their own compartments. Most of my current findings, charms and other miscellaneous supplies are in a storage container from the diy shop meant for screws and nails. It has multiple drawers that are transparent so I can see inside and it sits on my worktable for easy access.

tall order

Beads, sweets and other items are often sold in clear plastic tubes with replaceable lids, which make excellent bead stores. However, small tubes are generally best – imagine seeing a bead you want at the bottom of this tall tube!

Clear plastic bags are another excellent option. I keep all my beads and stones in Ziploc® bags and then place them in a drawer. As you can imagine, I have lots of beads! However, for my business, I design by season and I only keep beads that I'm currently working on within reach. All others get placed in another multi-drawer unit on the other side of the room.

storage tips

Here are some additional storage tips that I've picked up over the years:

• Clear containers such as aspirin bottles, Tic Tac® tubes, baby food jars, and clear bags are better than opaque ones because you can easily see the contents.

• If you want to use opaque storage, such as sweet tins, 35mm film holders or margarine containers, you can. To help you find what you are looking for, write the contents on the outside or take a photo of the contents and stick it to the lid for quick reference.

• You don't have to spend a lot of money on bead storage – I know you've already spent enough on the beads! Look around your house and garage to see what you may be able to recycle for your beading. I've even heard of someone converting their spice rack into a bead rack. Now that's creative!

resources

USA

Maya's choice:

Beads and Pieces
1320 Commerce St, Suite C,
Petaluma, CA 94954
Tel 800-652-3237
www.beadsandpieces.com
*Quality beads in wood, horn, shell,
glass, silver and gold, seed pods,
findings, tools and more*

The Beadin' Path
15 Main St
Freeport, ME 04032
Tel 207-865-4785
www.beadinpath.com
*Plenty of quality semi-precious stones
and pearls galore, other bead types,
finished jewellery, books and more*

The Bead Shop
Tel 650-386-6962
www.beadshop.com
*All sorts of beads including wood,
semi-precious, crystal and more,
charms, stringing materials, bags
and boxes available online only*

Earthstone
112 Harvard Ave #54
Claremont, CA 91711
Tel 800-747-8088
www.earthstone.com
*Massive array of semi-precious and
rare beads in a wide range of
shapes and sizes*

Fire Mountain Gems
1 Fire Mountain Way
Grants Pass, OR 97526-2373
Tel 800-355-2137
www.firemountaingems.com
*Beads of all types to suit all pockets,
findings, stringing materials, chain,
gold beads, tools, storage solutions
and instructions*

Fusion Beads
13024 Stone Ave N
Seattle, WA 98133
Tel 206-782-4595
www.fusionbeads.com
*Crystal, rhinestone, glass, wooden
and other beads, chain, findings
and much more*

Helby
37 Hayward Ave
Carteret, NJ 07008
Tel 732-969-5300
www.helby.com
*Supplier of Bead Smith tools plus
findings, stringing materials and
beads. Wholesale only*

Kings Beads
309 N Kings Road
Los Angeles, CA 90048
Tel 800-556-0194
www.kingsbeadsla.com
Semi-precious and other beads

Lucky Gems
1220 Broadway, 3rd Floor
New York, NY 10001
Tel 212-268-8866
www.lucky-gems.us
*Large array of pearls in many shapes
and colours, and wide range of
semi-precious beads*

Metalliferous, Inc

34 West 46th St
New York, NY 10036
Tel 212-944-0909
http://store.metalliferous.com
Semi-precious, crystal, glass, horn, plastic and other beads

Rio Grande

7500 Bluewater Road NW
Albuquerque, NM 87121
Tel 505-839-3011
www.riogrande.com
Said to be the largest and most complete supplier to the jewellery industry in the world, see their bead classes at the trade shows

Soft Flex Company

PO Box 80
Sonoma, CA 95476
Tel 707-938-3097
www.softflexcompany.com
Suppliers of fine-quality wire but also of beads, connectors and more

Taj Company

42 West 48th St 14th floor
New York, NY 10036
Tel 800-325-0825
www.tajco.com
Precious and semi-precious beads, pearls and metal beads

Toho Shoji

990 6th Ave
New York, NY 10018
Tel 212-868-7465
www.tohoshoji-ny.com
Variety of beads, wide range of findings including bead caps, clasps, earring parts and tools

Also try:

All Season Trading Co

888 Brannan #1160,
San Francisco, CA 94103
Tel 415-864-3308
www.allseason.com
Massive range of beads of many types including semi-precious, silver, glass and more, plus plenty of findings and components

Eastern Findings Corp

116 County Courthouse Road
Garden City Park, NY 11040
Tel 516-747-6640
www.easternfindings.com
Just about any finding you could think of and a massive range of chains, bracelets and more

Enchanting Beads

Michelle Hershman
PO Box 905
Lillian, AL 36549
www.enchantingbeads.com
Quality beads including semi-precious, pearls and lampwork

Holy Gemstone

1300 Peachtree Industrial Blvd
Suite 3210-3212
Suwance, GA 30024
Tel 678-482-8778
www.holygemstone.com
Semi-precious beads only, but a huge selection to choose from

New England Bead Exchange

12 Main St
Keene, NH 03431
Tel 603-352-7192
www.nebeads.com
Beads and beading classes

Silver Rose Beads

Tel 253-845-4949
www.silverrosebeads.com
Wonderful selection of semi-precious and metal beads plus details of the meanings of most stones

2 Bead or not 2 Bead

PO Box 565
Clifton Park, NY 12065-0565
Tel 866-733-5233
www.2beadornot2bead.com
Huge range of beads in most categories and plenty of findings including chain

Canada

Bead FX

128 Manville Road, Suit 9
Scarborough, ON M1L 4J5
Tel 416-701-1373
www.beadfx.com
Mainly glass and crystal beads plus some metal ones, findings, and lessons etc.

The Sassy Bead Co

11 William St
Ottawa, ON K1N 9C7
Tel 613-562-2812
or
757 Bank St
Ottawa, ON K1S 3V3
Tel 613-567-7886
www.thesassybeadco.com
Mainly glass and crystal beads plus some metal ones, findings and lessons etc.

UK

Bead Addict

8 Charter Close
Sale, Cheshire M33 5YG
Tel 0161-937-1945
www.beadaddict.co.uk
Semi-precious beads, unusual beads such as dichroic and Murano, fused glass, pearls, charms, pendants, findings including vermeil, and more

The Bead Shop

21A Tower St
Covent Garden
London WC2H 9NS
Tel 020-7240-0931
www.beadworks.co.uk
Wide range of beads to suit all pockets including range of semi-precious beads, findings of all descriptions

The Bead Shop (Nottingham)

7 Market St
Nottingham NG1 6HY
Tel: 0115-958-8899
www.mailorder-beads.co.uk
Beads in semi-precious stones, crystal, glass, ceramic, palmwood, and pearl, plenty of tools and more

Creative Beadcraft

1 Marshall St
London W1F 9BA
Tel 020-7734-1982
www.creativebeadcraft.co.uk
Wooden, plastic, glass and crystal beads, findings, kits, workshops and more

Little Beader

Novacraft
221 London Road
Rayleigh, Essex SS6 9DN
www.littlebeader.com
Glass, bone and wooden beads, gemstone chips, findings, stringing materials and more

Magpie Jewellery

Kyleakin
Isle of Skye IV41 8PQ
Tel: 015-9953-4979
www.magpiejewellery.net
Quality beads including unusual specimens

PJ Beads

583C Liverpool Road
Ainsdale, Southport PR8 3LU
Tel 01704-575-461
www.beads.co.uk
Beads, findings and tools for jewellery makers

Australia

Bead Inspired

PO Box 7309
Gladstone, QLD 4680
Tel 07-4978-1319
www.beadinspired.com
*Large range of beads and findings
including semi-precious, pearls,
wooden beads and more available
online only*

The Bead Tree

11 Roseberry Ave
Fullarton, SA 5063
Tel 08-8271-4977
www.thebeadtree.com.au
*Well-established store specializing in
a range of beads, pearls, sequins,
and jewellery findings*

Jewellery Beads Australia

PO Box 148
Kwinana, WA 6966
www.jewellerybeadsaustralia.com.au
*Plenty of semi-precious beads,
pearls, crystal, and more*

Unique Beads Australia

PO Box 246
Thornlie, WA 6988
www.uniquebeads.com.au
*Specializing in unusual beads from
around the world, but especially
South East Asia*

New Zealand

Bead Bazaar

14 George St
Palmerston North 4410
Tel 06-356-8612
*Lots of beads, including wood and
paua, and plenty of findings*

Beads You Need

611 Worcester St
Linwood, Christchurch 8006
Tel 0064-3-381-8363
*Mainly acrylic, glass and crystal
beads plus findings*

Beadz Unlimited

Corner Innes Road and Cranford St
St Albans, Christchurch
Tel 03-379-5126
www.beadzunlimited.com
*Large range of beads and findings to
suit most pockets*

St Beads Ltd

76 Tennyson St
Napier
Tel: 06- 835-4488
www.jewelleryonline.co.nz
Good range of beads

Magazines

Bead & Button

www.beadandbutton.com
*Large number of easy-to-follow
projects, tips and resources*

Bead Style

www.beadstylemag.com
*Bi-monthy magazine from the
publishers of Bead & Button.
Large number of projects suitable
for beginners*

Beadwork

Tel 760-291-1531 to subscribe
www.interweave.com/magazines/
*Projects including beadweaving,
artist profiles, news and resources*

Lapidary Journal

Tel 720-291-1531 to subscribe
www.jewelryartistmagazine.com
*News, resources and projects from
beginner to advanced level*

Other

Stella & Dot

Tel 800-920-5893
www.stelladot.com
*Jewellery to buy directly from the
website, or host your own trunk show*

index

acknowledgements

author's acknowledgements

I would like to thank the following:

• My mother and grandmother for allowing me to take apart their old jewellery.

• All my friends and family for their never ending support over the years.

• Kira Groneveldt for running my business while I was writing this book and Jesse Cromwell for doing everything else.

Thank you Tristan Brando, Kat Clare and Tom Hoberman. Thanks to everyone at DK publishing, particularly Shannon Beatty, Betsy Hosegood and Miranda Harvey.

Thank you to Janice Parsons from the The Bead Shop (Palo Alto), who helped me with the instructions for the Lovely lariat.

A big thank you also goes to Luxe Jewels (now Stella & Dot) for their help with this project and for motivating me to teach the world how to bead.

Last, but not least, I want to thank my husband, Scott, who believed in me and encouraged me to quit my full-time job to start my own jewellery business. And who continues to support me in every endeavour, even if it means being away from home.

And my children Jack and Sadie who inspire me every day and are always gentle with "mummy's necklaces".

publisher's acknowledgements

Dorling Kindersley would like to thank Gunilla Johansson, who, in addition to being a superb hand model, designed all the projects in the Quick & Easy section and who made many of the projects for this book.

Thanks also to the photographer, Ruth Jenkinson and her assistants Sarah Bailey, Anne and Danielle; Maia Terry for naming and archiving the digital photography files; and Kathie Gill for proofreading and indexing the book.

We would also like to thank the bead suppliers who either lent us items for photography or who sold them to us at a generous discount:

• Stella & Dot (formerly Luxe Jewels)

• Creative Beadcraft, London

• The Bead Shop, Covent Garden, London

project credits

Lucky green bracelet (pages 108–111) and Vintage multi-strand bracelet (pages 112–115) appear courtesy of Maya Brenner for Luxe Jewels (Stella & Dot).

picture credits

Page 7: Cyndi Finkle; all other images © DK Images.